"Danielle Walker understands the incredible power that food has to help and to heal. Her inviting, vibrant recipes welcome everyone to the table with generosity and deliciousness. That's something we can all celebrate!"

—MARK HYMAN, MD, *New York Times* best-selling author of *Eat Fat, Get Thin*

"Danielle is a master of her craft and this book is no exception. This is grain-free entertaining at its best and, most importantly, has the whole family in mind so no one is left out of an important celebration."

—LISA LEAKE, *#1 New York Times* best-selling author of *100 Days of Real Food*

"All of us form memories around food. So when we have to change our diet, it's easy to fear that we'll lose our ability to connect and take part in traditions. Danielle Walker understands this so well, and with 125 mouthwatering recipes, she proves that no matter what we eat (or don't eat), we never have to give up the joy of celebrating with food."

—ANDIE MITCHELL, *New York Times* best-selling author of
It Was Me All Along and *Eating in the Middle*

DANIELLE WALKER'S
AGAINST *all* GRAIN

Celebrations

DANIELLE WALKER'S
AGAINST all GRAIN

Celebrations

A year of gluten-free, dairy-free, and Paleo recipes
for every occasion

PHOTOGRAPHY BY
Erin Kunkel

TEN SPEED PRESS
Berkeley

contents

"This is the power of gathering: it inspires us—
delightfully—to be more hopeful, more joyful,
more thoughtful: in a word, more alive."

—ALICE WATERS

introduction: *celebrate with me*

Many of my fondest memories are tied to holidays. Most of those memories are woven into the food we enjoy during those special times of the year. I remember being taught how to prepare a Thanksgiving turkey for the first time (accidentally baking it with the bag of giblets inside the cavity!) and baking dozens of cookies from old family recipes with my sister and my mom to hand out to friends during Christmastime. I look forward to reuniting with family and friends at holiday gatherings and congregating around the table to enjoy wonderful food and conversation. I especially love time spent in the kitchen with everyone busily preparing their favorite holiday dishes and later laughing over a glass of wine while cleaning up the mess from the celebration.

When you are forced to alter your diet drastically for the sake of your health, you may understandably fear that your fond memories and traditions will be lost along with the newly eliminated food groups. You may worry that you won't be able to attend significant gatherings with your family or host a baby shower for a friend without feeling ostracized or, worse, hungry! There is also a deep sense of loss when you can no longer experience the joy that comes from lovingly preparing and serving food to the people you care about. Those fears were once very real to me and left me feeling hopeless. But I have since made it my mission, with my blog and with my books, to break the misconception that you have to live a life of deprivation and alienation when you adopt a new dietary lifestyle.

My initial switch to a grain-free and Paleo Diet came after spending many years battling for my life. I devoted months to seeing different specialists in an attempt to find out what was causing my symptoms and was told everything from "You're a hypochondriac" to "You might have colon cancer." After dozens of tests and many different doctors, I was ultimately diagnosed at the young age of twenty-two with ulcerative colitis, an incurable autoimmune disease that wrongfully attacks an otherwise healthy colon. I was devastated, and very lost. I was also newly married and had fairy-tale aspirations of having a beautiful family and of following in my mother's and grandmother's footsteps by hosting big parties year-round.

All of my doctors told me the same thing about my condition: diet did not cause it, diet cannot prevent it, and diet cannot cure it. So I accepted the myriad prescriptions and went on my way, only to have my symptoms worsen with burgeoning side effects. I spent years in and out of hospitals, incapacitated and on very high doses of medications. I was unable to be a mom to my infant son, and I took medical leave from my job. My sickness ruled my life until I discovered that dietary changes *could*, in fact, make my symptoms subside. I adopted a Paleo Diet, which is based on the types of foods presumed to have been eaten by early humans, before the agricultural revolution changed the way much of what we consume is grown and processed. It consists chiefly of grass-fed or pasture-raised proteins, fish, vegetables, fruit, seeds, nuts, and healthy fats, and it excludes dairy, legumes, grain products, and processed food. Many people who follow this lifestyle see improved blood lipids, weight loss, and a reduction or elimination of the symptoms associated with autoimmune diseases. (For an in-depth account of my health journey and the different stages I went through to find the Paleo Diet, read my blog at againstallgrain.com/my-journey or take a look at my first two cookbooks, *Against All Grain* and *Meals Made Simple*.)

After overhauling my diet, I spent quite some time avoiding parties and was apprehensive about hosting my own for fear that my guests would not enjoy the type of food I had to prepare. I was embarrassed to be a dinner guest with special requests and would often eat before leaving the house, or wait to eat until late at night when we returned home.

I will always remember my first Thanksgiving just weeks after switching to a Paleo Diet. I longingly looked at other diners' plates full of stuffing, mashed potatoes, and gravy; my plate had only turkey, salad, and a deflated, runny mashed cauliflower that I had brought for myself. Watching everyone enjoy all of the traditional pies and desserts after the meal was even more torturous. I debated between breaking my new "rules" or foregoing the special dishes I looked forward to year after year to preserve my health. I wondered if eating those foods, just this once, would affect me, but remembered from past experiences that it was not worth the risk.

It was after that disappointing dinner that I set out to re-create all of my favorite celebratory dishes in an attempt to give myself and my readers the gift of food traditions and to banish deprivation during holidays and special occasions. I forced myself to remember what had brought me joy before my diagnosis, and consciously committed to going against the grain in order to revive that joy.

I hosted my own Thanksgiving dinner the following year and proudly served all of my newly created recipes. My family and friends loved how fresh the food tasted. They even admitted that they felt better after the meal than in years past and didn't have the standard post-turkey fatigue. The next year, and every year after that, my guests arrived at my home for Thanksgiving bearing dishes cooked from my recipes. Although none of them had an autoimmune condition like I did, their love for me made them want to accommodate my diet. Beyond that, they continued to make my recipes for special events throughout the year and served them in place of the standard American classics.

reviving traditions

As I raise my own family, it is important to me that I share with them the same traditions and foods that I enjoyed growing up—but with our modified diet still in place. I want my sons to experience building and tasting gingerbread houses and to indulge in turkey-day favorites like creamy green bean casserole and apple pie. I want to preserve the tradition of making the pumpkin soup that my grandmother served every Halloween before we went trick-or-treating, and I want to wake up early to make a Valentine-themed breakfast just like my mom did every February 14. I want to bake cookies and serve hot cocoa with marshmallows to warm little bodies after a day of playing in the snow. I want to be able to throw my sons' birthday parties with foods that all of their buddies can enjoy, including a delicious grain-free cake to culminate the big event.

Trying new recipes that use unfamiliar ingredients can be a welcome adventure for some of you, but mostly I hear from my readers about how much anxiety it can bring. Playing with a new menu on a regular weeknight gives you some room for error, but the meal simply cannot fail when you have a table full of expectant guests celebrating a special holiday. That's why I transformed my most cherished family recipes and have collected them here. I tested each dish dozens of times to give you a book full of trustworthy recipes that you can feel confident serving, whether you are hosting a special guest with food allergies or cooking for a crowd of regular grain-eaters.

You will find mouthwatering dishes for twelve special occasions here, from a backyard barbecue to a full Christmas spread, to help you create a fabulous grain-free party that even your grain-eating friends will enjoy. I hope these recipes help you reestablish the joy of gathering and connecting around a table in community rather than allowing your different diet to isolate you. I also hope they restore nostalgia to your family celebrations and counter the fear that these traditions will be lost.

Remember, these recipes are not just for people following a grain-free diet; they will also appeal to anyone who wants to eat healthfully and share beautiful, entertaining inspiration with loved ones. These are my treasured food memories transformed. I invite you to join my family in finding happiness and satisfaction from making good food for friends and family and throwing an effortless and beautiful party.

getting started

If you are new to a grain-free or Paleo lifestyle, you'll find lots of information to help you make a smooth transition to this way of eating. The recipes include two special features, Make It Ahead and Tidbits, which are explained on page 4, along with other features of the book, including information on special diets, serving sizes, and on where to find nutritional data.

You'll also find tips on grain-free baking that I have developed through years of trial and error (see Grain-Free Recipe Guidelines, page 6). The section called Ingredient Glossary and Substitutions (page 12) will familiarize you with some of the unusual ingredients that go along with this way of eating. And Kitchen Gear (page 20) will help you stock your kitchen with the equipment that makes cooking and baking this food as easy as possible.

And finally, beginning on page 7, I share a few entertaining and preparation tips that might even make your everyday eating more effortless.

MAKE IT AHEAD

One of the most frequent questions I get from readers is whether or not a dish can be made ahead of time: Can this be frozen uncooked or already baked? Will this dough hold up if it's made a few days in advance? Making things ahead of time with grain-free cooking is quite similar to conventional cooking in terms of meat and produce, but the baking can be confusing for people new to the lifestyle. Grain-free and Paleo recipes require a bit more preparation than most people are used to because there are not many convenience items on the market, such as premade pie dough or tasty Paleo-friendly condiments, to make the prep go more quickly. When you are entertaining, you have the added task of planning the party, so anything that can be done in advance helps to relieve stress. I've added make-ahead notes at the bottom of many recipes, so be sure to read these a week before your party and before heading to the grocery store to plan ahead and get some tasks out of the way.

TIDBITS

I've been cooking grain-free since 2009 and have learned much along the way. As a blogger, I enjoy the interactions I have with you, my readers. I adore hearing about your health progress and, of course, about how my recipes were used in your home and during your celebrations. Although the volume of substitution requests or ingredient questions can sometimes be overwhelming, I try to respond to as many of them as possible because

I understand how daunting this way of cooking can seem at first. After all, your heirloom family cookbooks for conventional cooking are no longer of use, so I try to share my knowledge whenever I can.

Unfortunately, I'm not able to provide assistance as frequently or as immediately in a cookbook as I do in my blog, so I tried to anticipate all of your questions ahead of time and answered them in the Tidbits note at the end of the recipes. These are my personal tips, ranging from repurposing leftovers of a dish to which brands work best for particular recipes.

SPECIAL DIETS AND FOOD ALLERGIES

As if being on a grain-free diet weren't restrictive enough, there are many of us who have to be on even more modified diets or have food allergies. In addition to Paleo, many of you follow SCD (Specific Carbohydrate Diet) or GAPS (Gut and Psychology Syndrome Diet), or need egg-free, nut-free, or nightshade-free recipes. I have provided a table beginning on page 338 that lists my recipes according to these categories to help you plan the best menu for your individual needs.

NUTRITIONAL DATA

For those of you who are following special programs or watching your nutritional numbers for health reasons, I've provided nutritional information on my website for all of the recipes in the book. Find it online at CelebrationsCookbook.com/nutritional-data.

A NOTE ON SERVING SIZES

The serving sizes for the recipes in this book were determined with the assumption that a full party spread would be served family-style and everyone would take a little of each dish. Most of the menus serve eight, but for big

holidays like Thanksgiving—where there is a lot of cooking time involved—I scaled recipes up to serve ten to twelve so you can either feed a large crowd or reap the benefits of your labor with leftovers the following days.

grain-free recipe guidelines

The following tips hold true for all kinds of cooking but will be especially helpful in your grain-free baking endeavors. Eating Paleo isn't that difficult if you just eat meat and vegetables. On the other hand, grain-free baking is commonly a source of frustration for people new to this way of eating. There is a plethora of naturally grain-free and Paleo recipes available on popular food websites and in cookbooks. But what is harder to find is how to substitute arrowroot powder or almond flour for all-purpose flour in your great-grandmother's traditional thumbprint cookie recipe, or how many eggs to add to a recipe when you use coconut flour. You cannot call Martha or Ina and ask them how to make their Christmas fudge using Paleo ingredients, but you can very likely use their recipes for roasted turkey or fillet of beef without any substitutions at all.

I have dedicated much of my time to testing and perfecting recipes for traditional treats and sweets like gingersnaps and biscotti—so you can have success making these in your own kitchen without having to go through the trial-and-error process of converting an old recipe yourself. But before you start baking any of the recipes in this book, here are five lessons I have learned along the way to ensure success.

READ THE RECIPES IN THEIR ENTIRETY BEFORE STARTING.

This way you know if a piece of parchment paper needs to be cut and fitted into a baking pan, or if the eggs need to come to room temperature first. Baking soda, which is the most frequent leavening agent used in this book, reacts immediately upon hitting the acidic ingredients, so these batters need to get into the oven quickly. You do not want to leave your cake batter sitting on the counter while you fumble with parchment paper or wait for the oven to preheat.

BUY THE RIGHT INGREDIENTS.

I cannot stress enough how important it is to buy quality ingredients; if you can, purchase my recommended brands. I have tested my recipes with various brands of almond and coconut flour, as well as palm shortening and coconut sugar, and these products all vary greatly. While the recipes will work with any brand you are able to find at your market, the best quality and texture will come from using the brands I recommend.

If your baked goods are oily or crumbly, the usual culprit is the flour. The almond flour must be finely ground from blanched almonds (without skins). Coconut flour is very absorbent, so measure carefully and only use the amount called for in the recipe. If you would like to substitute an ingredient, please refer to the Ingredient Glossary and Substitutions section (page 12).

MEASURE YOUR INGREDIENTS *VERY* CAREFULLY.

I want this book to be accessible to everyone, whether you are a novice or a seasoned chef. I recognize that not everyone owns a kitchen scale or understands how to figure out ratios. There are conversion charts in the back of the book for those who prefer to bake by weight. Be sure to use a kitchen scale for weighing, and do not use the liquid measurements in fluid ounces found on glass measuring cups for nuts or flours.

For the purpose of these recipes, use the scoop-and-sweep method for measuring flour: fluff up the flour in your package with a fork, dip the cup or spoon into the flour to scoop it up, and then sweep the top level with the back of a knife. Do not pack it down. If you double a recipe that calls for coconut flour, I recommend measuring out the ingredients twice. This may sound tedious, but coconut flour is very finicky, and even an extra teaspoon can change the texture of a baked item.

I give weight measures instead of volume for whole raw cashews, raw cacao butter, and unsweetened chocolate bars because the ingredients need to be very accurate for the recipe to work or because the ingredient is likely to measure inconsistently based on the size of the pieces.

USE CAUTION WHEN SUBSTITUTING INGREDIENTS.

Many of these recipes were originally tested using different ingredients, and I ultimately landed on the combination as written because it was truly the best. That being said, I understand everyone has his or her own dietary needs or allergies and may need to swap things out here and there. While I cannot guarantee a perfect result without testing your substitutions rigorously, I have included a list of common baking substitutions that tend to work well in the Ingredient Glossary and Substitutions section (page 12). Keep in mind that the end product will vary from my original creation but will likely still be delicious!

BAKING AND COOLING TIMES MATTER—SERIOUSLY!

My mom has this funny quirk that compels her to open the oven door when she enters my house to smell whatever I'm making. I always snap at her to close the door! Don't open the oven until a few minutes before the timer goes off to ensure that the hot air stays inside and the cake bakes evenly. If you open too early, and especially if you pull the oven rack out, cakes and breads can deflate and collapse in the center. Similarly, baked goods need adequate time to cool. As tempting as it is to slice into a hot-from-the-oven cake or loaf of bread, let them sit for the directed amount of time to allow the flours to set and absorb some moisture. Baked goods made with coconut flour will seem overly moist and baked goods made with arrowroot will seem gummy if you try them when they're still warm. Practice patience and you will be rewarded.

top ten tips for effortless entertaining

In addition to the recipe-specific Make It Ahead tips provided throughout the book, here are my top ten tips for entertaining that will bring ease to your celebration preparation.

1. DECORATE IN ADVANCE.

If you are specially decorating for the event, get this out of the way as early as you can. Your decor does not need to be intricate: a few fresh flowers and lighted candles will make the table feel special. Use fresh herbs and twine to tie napkins and make the place settings look more fancy than every day, or borrow dinnerware from friends to set a quaintly mismatched table. Set your table a few days

before the gathering, have candles out and ready to be lit, and arrange flowers in vases two days beforehand so the blooms have time to open.

2. SET THE MOOD.

Music plays a big role in setting the mood. Look online through music services such as Spotify, Pandora, or Google Play for music playlists that will go with your theme. I'm not much of a music buff; I love to use already curated playlists so I don't have to fret about picking the right songs.

Some of my favorite music for an upbeat fête like New Year's Eve comes from compilations put out by Hôtel Costes. Wyndham Hill and Vince Guaraldi have much to choose from for a cozy Thanksgiving or festive Christmas dinner. And my default for an intimate Halloween dinner party or a romantic Valentine's Day dinner are classics from Frank Sinatra and Ella Fitzgerald. (I'm an old soul and my dad trained me well, what can I say?) Listen to the playlist in advance, maybe while you're doing the cooking and setting up, so you can delete any tracks you are not fond of. And be sure to purchase a subscription to the music service so you don't end up with pesky commercials playing!

3. DO YOUR HOMEWORK.

Read through the recipes you intend to make a week before the event. Make a grocery list: check to see what you have on hand and which items will be used multiple times. Read through the Make It Ahead and Tidbits notes to see if there are any tips that can help in your planning, and execute those ahead of time.

4. SHOP EARLY.

Don't try to do all of your shopping the day before or on the day of the event. You run the risk of something coming up that limits your time, or the store being out of stock of ingredients you need. Stock your house with nonperishable items like paper towels, toilet paper, garbage bags, and celebratory decor to limit the amount of items you need to buy when you should be focusing on cooking and to avoid having to send someone out during the party to replenish the basics. A week ahead, make sure your pantry items such as dried spices, baking soda, and arrowroot powder are all fresh. For groceries, shop two to three days in advance and prepare whatever you can as soon as you return from the market.

5. GET CHOPPING.

Peeling and chopping vegetables can be time-consuming, especially if you don't have the knife skills of an Iron Chef. I keep chopped garlic and onions in airtight containers in the refrigerator for five days at a time so they are always on hand to be thrown into a sauté pan. I use a food processor to save time—and my tears. Vegetables such as potatoes, carrots, celery, jicama, and cucumbers will maintain their crispness and color if they are chopped up and stored, tightly covered, in a bowl of water in the refrigerator. You can peel and cube winter squash, such as butternut or pumpkin, and store it in containers in the refrigerator as well. For chopped herbs and lettuces, wash and dry them well, then wrap them in a barely damp paper towel and store them in a plastic bag in the fridge for two to three days. Basil, cilantro, and mint tend to brown once chopped, so store these whole.

6. MAKE IT AHEAD.

Make sauces and condiments a couple of days in advance. Soups, casseroles, and most desserts can be made a couple of days in advance, too. Vegetables that will be roasted can be cubed, tossed in oil, and seasoned, then stored in the refrigerator for two days. For items that cannot be frozen or fully assembled in advance, there are many steps that you can get out of the way so you have more time to visit with your guests. Assemble salads without the dressing and keep them in the refrigerator for a few hours before serving, or season your meats the night before so they are ready to be cooked. Also, refer to the Make It Ahead tips provided with the recipes.

7. ORGANIZE YOUR SERVING WARE.

One thing I learned from my grandmother was to have a designated platter, serving dish, or cutting board for each item you plan to serve. One day beforehand, gather your serving dishes or borrow things you're missing from a friend or neighbor and lay them out on the counter with sticky notes giving the dish name so you know that everything has a place when you're ready to serve.

8. SET UP YOUR STATION.

When you are ready to start cooking, read through each recipe in its entirety again before getting started. Then, gather the ingredients and tools you need and set up your *mise en place* (this is a French phrase that means to have everything in its place). This will save you time and make the cooking process much more enjoyable, plus it will limit the surprises and "uh-ohs!" that happen while you cook. If you're using the same herb, onions, or garlic in two different dishes, you can chop it all up and distribute it as needed, rather than using and cleaning your kitchen tools twice.

9. ACCEPT HELP.

Holidays and birthdays are about bringing loved ones together around a table to celebrate momentous occasions. While consuming the meal and engaging in community is, of course, enjoyable, joy can also be found in the preparation and serving of the meal. Let others experience that joy with you, and give yourself a little break by having people bring dishes or help you cook in the kitchen. When you send out the invitation, it is perfectly acceptable to provide a list of the dishes you need people to contribute. Even giving someone the task of picking up ice and providing beverages can be a weight off your shoulders.

10. HAVE FUN!

Finally, and most important, have fun. This is a celebration, after all. Feel free to play with the menus and use recipes from a variety of chapters for any of your events. If you're attending a Thanksgiving dinner and have been assigned to bring an appetizer, take a look at some of the ideas from the New Year's Eve Cocktail Party (page 23), Game Day Buffet (page 47), or Summer Shower (page 183). If you would like to serve a salad for Thanksgiving, the Roasted Autumn Harvest Salad (page 223) or Persimmon Prosciutto Salad (page 276) would be lovely. Perhaps the main entrées of the Christmas dinner don't suit your traditions, and you are used to eating ham or turkey. The Blood Orange and Honey-Glazed Ham (page 98) or the Brined and Roasted Turkey (page 249) from the Thanksgiving chapter would be a nice addition.

Happy celebrating, my friends!

With love, from my family to yours,

ingredient glossary and substitutions

Below you will find a list of my commonly used pantry staples, with information on what they are and where to find them. The recipes in this book will have the best outcomes if they are made as written; however, I have also included substitution advice should you need to make swaps to fit your needs.

New products are always coming on the market, and I am lucky to be among the first to hear about most of them. Many of my favorite products are listed on my website, againstallgrain.com, or look for them through online retailers Amazon, Vitacost, TropicalTraditions.com, and ThriveMarket.com.

ALMOND FLOUR is made from blanched (skinned) almonds that are finely ground into flour. The finer the grind, the better your baked goods will turn out. Coarsely ground flour, which is the type most commonly found in grocery stores, or homemade almond flour results in overly moist products that will sink in the center or have a grainy texture. I suggest purchasing almond flour from my trusted brands for the best results. If you're a frequent baker, store 1 pound of almond flour in a sealed container at room temperature and put the rest in a sealed container in the refrigerator for 1 month or in the freezer for 6 months.

Finely ground cashew flour can be substituted in a 1:1 ratio, but use the weight conversions on page 333 instead of the volume measurements listed in the recipe. To make a recipe nut-free, substitute finely ground raw sunflower seeds in a 1:1 ratio, but add 1 teaspoon lemon juice or apple cider vinegar and decrease the baking soda by half to prevent the baked good from turning green.

Sources: WellBee's brand (Wellbees.com, Amazon), Honeyville brand (Honeyville.com, Amazon, or occasionally at Costco), and Yupik brand Almond Powder (only available in Canada at some health food stores or through Amazon.ca).

ALMOND MEAL is similar to almond flour, but it is coarser and the skins have generally not been removed. It works wonderfully for breading fish and poultry and as a bread crumb substitute, but does not work well in baked goods. Almond meal can be purchased in stores or online, but it can also be made at home by grinding whole raw almonds in a food processor until you have a coarse, sandlike texture. Don't overprocess or you'll end up with almond butter.

Sources: Trader Joe's brand and Bob's Red Mill brand (found at Whole Foods and through online retailers; this is packaged as almond flour/meal and won't work well for the baking recipes that use blanched almond flour because it is too coarse, but it will work as a breading or bread crumb substitute).

ARROWROOT POWDER is made from the starchy arrowroot plant and is used as a substitute for cornstarch and potato starch. It helps to give breads and cakes a nice crumb and is a wonderful gluten-free ingredient for baking or thickening when there are tree nut and coconut allergies. It is not the same as tapioca starch, which comes from the cassava root and is not as easily digested, but it can be substituted in a 1:1 ratio. Although not Paleo, other grain-free starches, such as potato starch, can also be used in place of arrowroot powder.

Sources: Starwest Botanicals brand (organic arrowroot powder available through online retailers or in some health food stores) and Bob's Red Mill brand (found at most grocery stores and through online retailers).

BAKING SODA and BAKING POWDER are often confused for each other but are not the same. Since many store-bought baking powders contain grain-based starches, make your own at home using the recipe on page 325 to keep it grain-free, or look for Hain's brand, which uses potato starch instead of cornstarch. Purchase your baking soda at any grocery store. Make sure both are fresh to give your dishes the optimal texture.

Source: Hain's gluten-free Featherweight Baking Powder (found at health food stores and through online retailers).

CACAO BUTTER is the pure oil extracted from the cacao bean. I call for raw cacao butter throughout the book either as an emulsifier or to add moisture to baked goods. I also combine it with cocoa powder to make crisp chocolate shells in my Halloween chocolate candies (see page 210) and New Year's Eve Champagne Chocolate Strawberries (page 40). A 1-pound bag stored in the refrigerator will last for 6 months.

Sources: Navitas Naturals brand (found at most health food stores or through online retailers), The Raw Food World brand (found through online retailers), and Artisana brand (found at health food stores and through online retailers).

CASHEWS contain about the same amount of protein and fat as almonds but their flavor is very neutral, and they add a velvety texture to dishes. I use whole raw cashews frequently as a substitute for heavy cream in soups or sauces or even to make whipped cream (page 332). I also use cashew milk (page 324) as a dairy milk substitute and reach for it instead of almond milk (page 320) if I'm looking for creamy richness. If you cannot tolerate cashews but can handle dairy, you will have good results substituting grass-fed cream. In recipes for baked goods that call for whole raw cashews, you may also use macadamia nuts or blanched almonds. Refer to the weight conversions on page 333 instead of the volume measurements listed in the recipe, since equal volumes of nuts do not weigh the same.

Sources: Nuts.com, Costco, Trader Joe's, and Whole Foods.

CASHEW FLOUR is similar to almond flour but is made from finely ground raw cashews. It can be found commercially, but it can also be made at home by grinding raw cashews in a spice grinder or food processor and sifting out any large fragments. Cashew flour provides a neutral flavor and fluffy texture for baked goods. See the almond flour entry (opposite page) for how to substitute other nuts and for nut-free suggestions.

Sources: WellBee's brand (Wellbees.com, Amazon, and other online retailers) and Trader Joe's brand.

CHIA SEEDS are rich in omega-3 fatty acids and antioxidants and are used as a binding agent, thickener, or egg substitute in some of my recipes. I prefer to use ground white chia seeds because they don't affect the color of a dish, but that is simply my preference, and black chia seeds can be used interchangeably.

Sources: Nutiva brand (found in most health food stores, at Costco, and through online retailers) and Terrasoul Superfoods (found through online retailers).

CHOCOLATE is one of my favorite sweet treats. I use unsweetened (100 percent cocoa) chocolate bars or cocoa powder and sweeten it naturally as often as possible. This way I can avoid processed sweeteners, soy lecithin, or dairy. Occasionally, I call for dark chocolate and like to use varieties that contain more than 80 percent cacao to keep the sugar content low. Thankfully, there are quite a few brands on the market that you can find in natural food stores or online that use unrefined sweeteners such as coconut or maple sugar. Read the labels to ensure your chocolate is free of soy, dairy, and gluten.

Sources: Guittard brand (100 percent unsweetened chocolate bars, found in natural food stores or online), eatingevolved.com (fair-trade, maple- and coconut sugar–sweetened dark chocolate bars), Equal Exchange (fair-trade dark chocolate chips and bars, found through online retailers and sometimes in natural food stores), and Enjoy Life brand (mini chocolate chips or chunk-style chocolate chips free of soy, gluten, dairy, and nuts; found through online retailers or grocery stores).

COCOA POWDER is used in two different forms in this book. When using cocoa powder, I differentiate between "natural cocoa powder," a nonalkalized cocoa powder, and "Dutch-processed cocoa powder," which is treated with an alkali to neutralize acidity. Although I use Dutch-processed cocoa to achieve a deep chocolate color and flavor in a couple of recipes, I mostly call for natural cocoa powder because it's made from cold-pressed cacao beans, has more nutritional benefits, and is higher in antioxidants than Dutch-processed cocoa powder. Try to use the type of cocoa powder I call for in the recipe, if possible. Substituting one for the other can alter the way the baked goods look, taste, and rise.

Sources: Equal Exchange (fair-trade, organic cocoa powder, found in natural food stores and through online retailers) and Rapunzel brand (Dutch-processed cocoa powder, found in natural food stores and through online retailers).

COCONUT AMINOS is made from naturally aged coconut sap blended with sea salt and is a soy- and gluten-free soy sauce substitute. It is wonderful in Asian cuisine or to add a salty flavor to sauces and marinades. Use coconut aminos just like you would soy sauce, but add a dash of sea salt since it is a bit sweeter.

Source: Coconut Secret brand (found in natural food stores and through online retailers).

COCONUT BUTTER, also known as coconut manna or coconut cream concentrate, is made by blending whole coconut flesh. I use it as a thickener in some recipes and also to make dessert glazes and frostings, like in the Cutout Cookies frosting (page 318) and Lemon Lavender Bundt Cakes (page 197). Before using, be sure to stir the oil fully into the flesh and to warm the jar slightly to make it soft enough to stir if needed.

Sources: TropicalTraditions.com (calls it coconut cream concentrate) and Nutiva brand (calls it coconut manna, found in natural food stores and through online retailers).

COCONUT FLOUR is made by dehydrating and finely grinding the meat of a coconut. It is packed with dietary fiber and protein and is a naturally gluten-free flour alternative. The high-fiber content also keeps sugars from being absorbed into the bloodstream. It is a great alternative for those with tree-nut or wheat allergies, but can be somewhat tricky to bake with because it is extremely absorbent. Even an extra teaspoon can yield a different result in a baked product. Because of its absorbency, recipes using coconut flour rely on eggs or added moisture for volume and a very small amount of the flour is used compared to traditional flours. I do not suggest substituting coconut flour for nut flours because they have very different properties. If you bake frequently, store 8 ounces of coconut flour in a sealed container at room temperature, and store the rest in a sealed container in the refrigerator for up to 1 month or in the freezer for up to 6 months.

Sources: TropicalTraditions.com and Nutiva brand (found in most natural food stores, at Costco, and through online retailers).

COCONUT MILK is made by pureeing the meat and water from a coconut. Avoid the boxed coconut milk beverages typically sold in the refrigerated section of grocery stores; they contain additives and stabilizers to retain a liquid consistency. Instead, look for canned coconut milk (in BPA-free cans) that contains only coconut and water (which I refer to as full-fat coconut milk) and is preferably free of guar gum, to which some people are sensitive. Cashew milk can be substituted for coconut milk in recipes because it has a similar consistency and fat content. Cashew milk will not work, however, for recipes using only the cream from the can of coconut milk or for whipped coconut cream (page 331). When using a can of coconut milk, run it under warm water for a few minutes to soften the coconut cream, then shake the can vigorously to combine the cream and the water before using.

Sources: Natural Value brand (found in most natural food stores or through online retailers), Native Forest brand (works the best for my whipped coconut cream recipe; found through online retailers, at natural food stores, and occasionally at Trader Joe's), and Whole Foods 365 Organic brand (also works great for the whipped coconut cream recipe).

COCONUT OIL is a healthy fat that is extracted from the meat of the coconut. It has many medicinal properties and is used in food as well as skin-care products. It is heat stable, slow to oxidize, and resistant to rancidity, making it suitable for high-temperature cooking and frying. Coconut oil can be used in place of ghee or butter. I do not recommend using it in recipes that call for palm shortening because it will not produce the same texture or rise. Purchase organic virgin coconut oil for the recipes in this book. I occasionally call for expeller-pressed coconut oil, sometimes labeled unscented or unflavored coconut oil, because it goes through a steam deodorizing process so the taste is neutral, unlike virgin coconut oil, which retains the scent and taste of fresh coconuts.

Sources: TropicalTraditions.com, Nutiva brand (found in most natural food stores, at Costco, and through online retailers), Artisana brand (found in most natural food stores, at Costco, and through online retailers), and MaraNatha brand (found in most natural food stores and through online retailers).

COCONUT SUGAR, also known as coconut crystals or palm sugar, is produced from the sap of the flower buds of the coconut palm tree. It has been used as a traditional sweetener for thousands of years and is similar to brown sugar in taste and color. Coconut sugar can be substituted in a 1:1 ratio for maple sugar, but it will give the dish a deeper amber color and a less sweet flavor.

Sources: Trader Joe's brand and Nutiva brand (found in natural food stores, at Costco, and through online retailers).

EGGS are used in my baking recipes to bind and give rise to cookies, cakes, and breads. I use large eggs from pasture-raised organic hens. Although I have not tested each recipe in the book using egg swaps, I have found that recipes calling for three or fewer eggs can often be made with flaxseed, chia, or gelatin instead. Recipes for making these egg substitutes can be found online.

Sources: Vital Farms Pastured Eggs (found in natural food stores and sometimes at Costco), or organic eggs from a local farm or farmers' market.

EXTRA-VIRGIN OLIVE OIL is cold pressed and not exposed to heat, making it lower in linoleic acid (omega-6). Be sure to purchase brands packaged in dark bottles and keep the oil in a cool place when not in use. Though I opt to use ghee for high-heat cooking, I recommend extra-virgin olive oil as a dairy-free alternative for sautéing and, of course, for salads and other cold dishes. If olive oil is used to sauté or roast vegetables that give off a lot of water, like zucchini, there is less of a chance that it will reach its smoke point and oxidize. It can also be mixed with another high-heat fat to further

minimize the chances. Be sure to purchase 100 percent extra-virgin olive oil; many store-bought brands are mixed with lower quality oils.

Sources: Lucini Organic (found through online retailers) and Kirkland Organic brand (found at Costco and through online retailers).

FLAXSEED is a great source of dietary fiber and essential omega-3 fatty acids, and I occasionally use it as an egg substitute or to give a recipe the texture of bread crumbs. I prefer to use golden flaxseed to keep the color of my dishes lighter, but dark flaxseed can be used interchangeably.

Sources: Bob's Red Mill brand (found in natural food stores and through online retailers) and Whole Foods 365 Organic brand.

GELATIN is a fantastic thickener and binder, especially for desserts. I buy grass-fed gelatin online from Vital Proteins brand, but the unflavored Knox or Great Lakes brand found at standard grocery stores will work as well. Gelatin offers many health benefits for the gut, hair, and nails. Kosher fish gelatins, often available in natural food stores or found online, are good alternatives for those who prefer them for religious or personal reasons. Be sure to purchase the cold, water-insoluble kind of gelatin for these recipes. Cold, water-soluble gelatin, or hydrolyzed collagen, is great for smoothies or to stir into tea to add collagen to your diet, but it won't gel desserts such as my Vanilla Buttercream (page 160) or Berry Tart with Vanilla Bean Custard (page 178).

Sources: Vital Proteins brand (found through online retailers) and Great Lakes brand (found in natural food stores and through online retailers).

GHEE is clarified butter, which means the milk solids have been almost entirely removed, leaving only the healthy butterfat behind. Very pure ghee is 99 percent pure butter oil but may have trace amounts of casein and lactose. Unless you are extremely sensitive, it does not normally cause problems, even if other dairy does. Unsalted butter or palm shortening can be substituted for ghee in baked goods, and olive oil or coconut oil can be substituted in savory dishes. Ghee can be prepared easily at home (page 325) or purchased ready-made.

Sources: Pure Indian Foods brand (found through online retailers) and Purity Farms brand (found in many natural food stores and through online retailers).

HONEY is the sweetener I use most often. Raw, organic honey has many health benefits. It is both an energy and an immune booster and can greatly help with seasonal allergies, if you purchase it locally. Honey also contains mainly glucose and fructose, which are monosaccharides (single sugars) that are easy for the body to absorb and process. I suggest using a raw, light-colored honey such as clover for the baked goods, beverages, and frostings in this book. Light-colored honey will produce the correct color and texture, and it also has a mild flavor and won't overtake the flavor of the dish.

Sources: Local raw clover honey from your farmers' market or natural foods store, TropicalTraditions.com, and YS Organic brand (found in natural food stores and through online retailers).

MAPLE SUGAR is a granulated sugar made from the sap of the maple tree. It can be made at home using any of the various recipes found online or purchased commercially. Maple sugar can be substituted in a 1:1 ratio for coconut sugar, but it will lend a sweeter maple flavor to the dish.

Source: Coombs Family Farms brand (maple sugar and pure maple syrup, found in natural food stores and through online retailers).

MAPLE SYRUP is a natural, unrefined liquid sweetener that I often use to enhance the flavors of baked goods and savory dishes. Use pure grade A or B maple syrup or substitute honey in a 1:1 ratio, if desired.

Sources: Various brands at Costco, Trader Joe's, and Whole Foods, and Coombs Family Farms brand (found in natural food stores and through online retailers).

NUT MILKS are made from almonds, cashews, and other nuts, and are dairy-free alternatives to cow's milk. My recipes for almond milk and cashew milk are on pages 320 and 324, respectively, but store-bought nut milks can be used to save time. Always buy the unsweetened original flavor and look for brands with the fewest ingredients and no carrageenan or gums.

PALM SHORTENING is what I use as a butter substitute in my baked goods recipes. It has a firm texture and a high melting point, which creates fluffy, cakelike delights. It is not hydrogenated and contains no trans fats, making it a great dairy-free baking fat. Be sure to purchase this oil from sustainable and eco-friendly sources. Grass-fed unsalted butter or ghee, when noted on the individual recipe, can be used as a substitute, if you tolerate dairy. When a recipe calls for softened palm shortening, it should be at room temperature and have the consistency of softened butter. If the temperature in your kitchen runs cold, slightly warm the palm shortening container under warm running water for a few minutes.

If you are baking in the heat of the summer and the shortening is liquid, place the desired amount in the refrigerator for 30 minutes before baking.

Sources: TropicalTraditions.com and Spectrum Organics brand (usually labeled as vegetable shortening, found in many grocery stores or through online retailers).

SUNFLOWER FLOUR is made from grinding raw hulled sunflower seeds and can be used in place of almond flour or cashew flour to make items nut-free. You can find it online or make it at home by grinding the seeds in a coffee or spice grinder. For best results, before using, make sure the flour is very finely ground and sifted to remove any large particles. In my experience, a food processor does not get it fine enough. Beware, the chlorophyll in the seeds can react with baking soda and cause baked goods to turn a bright green. Fun for St. Patrick's Day but maybe not for day-to-day lunches. You can counter this reaction by adding a little fresh lemon juice, vinegar, or cream of tartar to the batter and reducing the baking soda by half.

Source: Eat Seeds brand (Eatseeds.com or Amazon).

SUNFLOWER SEED BUTTER, also known as sunbutter, is made from sunflower seeds and is a great alternative to almond butter for those with nut allergies. Look for brands that do not contain added sugars or oils.

Source: SunButter brand (unsweetened sunflower seed butter, found in natural food stores and through online retailers).

kitchen gear

If you are just beginning to venture back into the kitchen after fleeing with the anxiety that comes with a new dietary lifestyle, go through this list of my essential kitchen equipment and stock your cupboards with everything you need to help make your new foray into grain-free cooking enjoyable. You may be surprised by how many tools you already have, and the rest you can find at a discount on Amazon or through stores like Costco or HomeGoods. Otherwise, ask your family for gift certificates for birthdays and holidays and save up to get the things you still need.

In addition to the specialty items below, be sure to have all of the general kitchen items on hand, like rubber spatulas, balloon and small flat whisks, liquid measuring cups, flat-bottom dry measuring cups, measuring spoons, a colander, vegetable peeler, instant-read thermometer, a set of mixing bowls, a rolling pin, and parchment paper.

Here are a few favorite tools that every grain-free kitchen needs. Find my favorite brands at againstallgrain.com/shop.

baking equipment

BAKING SHEETS

Have two or three rimmed baking sheets in a variety of sizes for roasting vegetables or meats. For cookies, light-colored metal baking sheets without a rim work best for even baking of items containing nut flour. Airbake, or insulated, sheets are less likely to overheat or burn.

CAKE PANS

Keep two 6 by 2-inch and two 9 by 2-inch cake pans on hand for baking the birthday cakes in this book. Grain-free cakes are pretty dense and rich, so I like to make layered 6-inch cakes, which stand tall, look beautiful, and can easily feed eight people.

CANDY THERMOMETER

Several dessert recipes, including Caramel Apples (page 213) and Marshmallows (page 316), require a candy thermometer for the best results. They can be bought at any kitchen store.

LOAF PAN

A 10 by 4½-inch metal or silicone loaf pan gives the best results for my blender bread (page 323).

MUFFIN PAN

I prefer a 12-cavity silicone muffin pan, but also keep a 24-cavity mini muffin pan on hand.

PIE PLATE

Have two 9-inch and one 10-inch pie plate for the Thanksgiving pies (see pages 256 and 259) and Caramel-Pecan Sticky Buns (page 88).

small appliances

BLENDER

A high-speed blender can save you a lot of time. I use mine to create smooth batters, puree soups, and whip up smoothies. It is needed to crush whole raw cashews for my blender bread (page 323) and to make cake batters using nut flours as smooth as those made with conventional flour. Standard blenders will work for these recipes as well, but you may have to stop the blender and scrape down the sides a few times to get a smooth batter.

FOOD PROCESSOR

This machine can chop or grate vegetables and fruits, grind whole nuts, and puree cooked vegetables. Most models have a greater capacity than blenders and therefore offer more versatility in food preparation. If you need to choose between a blender and a food processor for budget or kitchen space reasons, I recommend choosing a high-speed blender over a food processor. My recipes that call for a food processor can often be made in a high-speed blender, but not vice versa because the food processor blade is larger than the blender blade and cannot yield as smooth a texture.

IMMERSION BLENDER

This handheld blender really comes in handy for making homemade mayonnaise (page 328), super-creamy deviled eggs (page 187), and for blending hot soups directly in the pot. It's not a necessity, but it is a nice addition to a grain-free kitchen.

SLOW COOKER

A slow cooker, or Crock-Pot, is incredibly handy for a busy cook and is also helpful for keeping dishes warm during a party, like my game-day Sweet-and-Sour Meatballs (page 50) or Carnitas on Tostones (page 57). I use a 6½-quart slow cooker, and recommend getting a model that is proportionately wide and shallow rather than narrow and deep for even cooking. This size also works really well when you want to double a recipe.

STAND MIXER

This works wonders when it comes to beating my Vanilla Buttercream (page 160), making Marshmallows (page 316), or preparing cookie dough. While a stand mixer is convenient and doesn't require any manual labor, an electric handheld mixer takes up less kitchen space and will get the job done at a fraction of the cost.

knives

Eating a whole foods diet entails quite a bit more preparation than a processed foods diet, so having a good set of sharp knives is a must. I saved up to purchase my knives one at a time, but it was well worth it. I use the Japanese brand Shun, but Wusthof and J.A. Henckels knives are reputable brands that are more affordable. All home cooks should have a 5½-inch Santoku knife, which has a dimpled edge that allows slices to slide off the knife without shredding, a paring knife, a carving knife, and a serrated knife in their arsenals. Have your knives professionally sharpened at least twice a year; check your local farmers' market for a knife-sharpening booth or take them to your closest kitchen supply store.

pots and pans

Although not inexpensive, my favorite pots and pans are made by Le Creuset. They're produced with nontoxic materials, heat quickly and evenly, will last a lifetime, and are easy to clean. Stainless-steel pots are also wonderful, and you can usually find whole sets discounted at stores like Costco or HomeGoods. It is useful to have at least a 2-quart saucepan with lid, a 10-inch skillet, an 8-quart stockpot, a 5-quart Dutch oven, and a roasting pan on hand.

new year's eve
cocktail party

◆◆◆

*Apple Parsnip
Soup Shooters*

*Oysters with Champagne-
Pomegranate Mignonette*

*Prosciutto-Wrapped
Glazed Shrimp*

*Spinach Artichoke Dip
with Crudités*

*Thai Chicken Meatballs
with Tamarind Chile Sauce*

Crab-Stuffed Mushrooms

◆◆◆

*Champagne Chocolate
Strawberries*

◆◆◆

Holiday Gimlet

NYE 75

Truth be told, since my husband, Ryan, and I became parents, we have fallen asleep long before the clock strikes midnight. We live on the West Coast, but we say "Happy *New York* New Year" at 9:00 p.m., when the ball drops on the East Coast, and then kiss goodnight. However, in our earlier years, and hopefully again once our little guys are older, I loved to throw a New Year's Eve cocktail soiree. With all of the buzz and excitement of the approaching New Year, a menu of bite-size appetizers and two signature cocktails—accompanied by Champagne, of course—is simple yet elegant.

When people are nibbling (and drinking) all night long, they tend to eat more than they would at a sit-down dinner, so all of these recipes are designed to serve a party of ten, or three to four pieces per person. I like to have a menu of mostly hearty, warm appetizers so my guests don't go home feeling like they still need to eat dinner. With this menu, your guests will ring in the New Year with delicacies such as stuffed mushrooms, oysters on the half shell, Thai meatballs wrapped in lettuce cups and dressed with a tangy, spicy sauce, and warm spinach artichoke dip. Plus they can sip and celebrate with two signature cocktails.

My brother, Joel, is the resident mixologist at every family party, so I asked him to help me create two special cocktails to ring in the New Year—a festive red gimlet punch, and a twist on a traditional French 75, which is a cocktail made from gin, lemon juice, and sugar and topped with bubbly. Traditional cocktail shakers only make three or four drinks at a time, so I added notes to each recipe telling you how to mix and serve these drinks to a crowd of ten if you do not want to be chained to the bar all night.

A little tip to keep the food fresh and ever flowing: When you're serving warm hors d'oeuvres that people will be snacking on all evening long, serve them in batches. Fill your platters with a portion of the appetizers, then cover and keep the remaining food warm in a 200°F oven. Replenish the trays as needed.

Whether you're using these recipes for the big transition into January, an elegant engagement party, or as starters for a festive holiday dinner, I hope your cocktail party is a smashing success with plenty of great food, delicious drinks, and happy friends and family.

Happy New Year!

apple parsnip soup shooters

Apples are crisp and tart and give this soup a nice zing that complements the Champagne that is likely flowing all evening long. And the pureed cauliflower and parsnips make this soup rich and creamy without the use of heavy cream, so you can enjoy it even after the healthy eating resolutions have begun. These are small servings, so I like to make enough for each guest to have a few shooters.

SERVES 10

2 tablespoons ghee (page 325) or coconut oil

2 shallots, peeled and diced

4 cloves garlic, minced

1 pound parsnips, peeled and diced

1 cup cauliflower florets

1 tart apple, peeled and diced, plus 1 tart apple, peeled and minced

6 cups chicken stock (page 327)

1 cup apple cider

½ teaspoon ground nutmeg

2 teaspoons fine sea salt

½ teaspoon freshly ground black pepper

1 teaspoon ground cinnamon

Heat 1 tablespoon of the ghee in a Dutch oven or deep pot set over medium heat. Add the shallots and garlic and sauté for 2 to 3 minutes, until translucent and fragrant. Add the parsnips, cauliflower, and the diced apple and continue cooking for 5 minutes, or until the vegetables have browned slightly. Add the chicken stock, apple cider, nutmeg, salt, and pepper. Bring to a boil, then reduce the heat to a simmer and cook for 15 minutes, or until the vegetables are soft. Working in batches, transfer the mixture to a blender and carefully blend until smooth. Return the soup to the pot and keep it warm over low heat.

Combine the remaining 1 tablespoon ghee, the minced apple, and cinnamon in a skillet set over medium-high heat. Sauté for 5 to 7 minutes, until the apple is crisp-tender.

To serve, ladle the soup into 10 tall shot glasses and top with a bit of the cinnamon-apple mixture. Keep the remaining soup warm in the pot set over low heat and the apple topping at room temperature. Replenish the tray of shot glasses as needed throughout the night.

make it ahead Make the soup and the cinnamon apple topping 3 days in advance and store them separately in tightly sealed containers. Reheat both components over medium-low heat before serving. To freeze, refrigerate the soup until it is cool, then freeze in an airtight container for 3 months. Thaw in the refrigerator overnight, then reheat in a saucepan over medium-low heat.

tidbits Use crisp and tart, but not sour, apples such as Fuji or Honeycrisp for the best flavor.

When blending a hot liquid, remove the plug from the blender top and cover it with a cloth towel to allow steam to escape and prevent splattering.

oysters with champagne-pomegranate mignonette

To make these oysters special and festive for ringing in the New Year, I use champagne vinegar and pomegranate juice in a classic mignonette (vinegar sauce) that is spooned over them. If you're an oyster-phobe, try to remember while slurping them down that they are packed with protein and loaded with zinc, selenium, and iron. If that doesn't help, I'm sure there's an oyster lover in the room who will gladly take your share.

SERVES 10

2 tablespoons champagne vinegar

1 tablespoon pure pomegranate juice

1 teaspoon finely minced shallot

Fine sea salt and freshly ground black pepper

3 dozen fresh oysters, scrubbed, shucked, and left on the half shell

Fresh pomegranate seeds and fennel fronds, for garnish

Stir the vinegar, pomegranate juice, shallot, salt, and pepper together in a bowl. Set aside for 1 hour to allow the shallot to soften slightly.

Place the oysters on a platter set over a bed of crushed ice and serve with the mignonette on the side for spooning over the top. Garnish with pomegranate seeds and fennel fronds.

make it ahead Mix up the mignonette sauce up to 3 days in advance and store it in an airtight container in the refrigerator.

tidbits Look for oysters with tightly closed shells. If washing and shucking oysters seems daunting, ask your store's fishmonger to do it for you. Most will oblige. Be sure to serve fresh oysters within 1 to 2 days of purchase.

Rather than buying expensive bottles of pomegranate juice or concentrate, use a citrus juicer to extract the juice from ¼ cup pomegranate seeds.

Use the leafy fronds from the top of the fennel bulb used in the Spinach Artichoke Dip with Crudites (page 35) for this garnish.

prosciutto-wrapped glazed shrimp

A simple shrimp cocktail is delicious and festive, but the cocktail sauce is often made with high-fructose corn syrup, sugar, and starch. Instead, take this old favorite up a level with a savory and sweet glaze made from dried apricots and pure maple syrup. Crispy prosciutto is wrapped around the shrimp before baking, balancing the sweet sauce with a bit of saltiness.

SERVES 10

½ cup dried unsulfured apricots

1¼ cups water

¼ cup pure maple syrup

½ teaspoon chili powder

¼ teaspoon cayenne pepper

2 pounds jumbo raw shrimp (about 40 pieces), peeled and deveined with tails on

8 ounces prosciutto, sliced into thin ribbons

Preheat the oven to 425°F. Line a baking sheet with parchment paper.

To make the glaze, combine the apricots in a saucepan with ¾ cup of the water, the maple syrup, chili powder, and cayenne. Bring to a boil and simmer for 10 minutes, or until most of the liquid has evaporated and the apricots are rehydrated.

Transfer the mixture to a blender and add the remaining ½ cup water. Blend until smooth.

Wrap each shrimp with prosciutto and place, seam side down, on the baking sheet. Brush with the glaze.

Bake for 10 to 12 minutes, until the shrimp are opaque throughout. Brush again with the glaze midway through. Serve hot.

make it ahead These are best cooked and served immediately, but you can wrap the shrimp the day before and store them in the refrigerator. The sauce can be made up to 1 week ahead of time and stored in the refrigerator; check that off of your list early to reduce your pre-party stress.

spinach artichoke dip with crudités

You can serve this warm and creamy dip as an hors d'oeuvres for any occasion, but I've found it is always appreciated at a cocktail party. A creamy cashew sauce takes the place of cream cheese or grated cheese in this dish. Instead of a traditional baguette, make this a lot healthier by serving it with fresh raw vegetables, toasted grain-free blender bread (page 323), or store-bought sweet potato or taro chips.

SERVES 10

½ cup (about 70g) whole raw cashews

2 tablespoons ghee (page 325) or extra-virgin olive oil

1 cup diced yellow onion

½ cup chopped fennel bulb

4 cloves garlic, minced

1 cup water

2 teaspoons fine sea salt

1 teaspoon freshly ground black pepper

1 teaspoon garlic powder

½ teaspoon freshly squeezed lemon juice

½ teaspoon apple cider vinegar

¼ teaspoon cayenne pepper

1¼ pounds baby spinach

2 (14-ounce) cans water-packed artichoke hearts

¼ cup mayonnaise (page 328)

Fresh raw vegetables, such as carrots, endive, green beans, or thinly sliced radishes, for serving

Place the cashews in a bowl and cover them with boiling water. Soak them for 1 hour, then drain and rinse. Preheat the oven to 400°F.

Melt the ghee in a skillet set over medium-high heat. Add the onion, fennel, and garlic and sauté for 5 to 7 minutes, until the onion is translucent and aromatic.

Combine the cashews with the water in a blender. Add the sautéed onion mixture, salt, pepper, garlic powder, lemon juice, vinegar, and cayenne and blend until very smooth and thick. Pour into a bowl and set aside.

Bring a large pot of water to a boil. Add the spinach and cook until bright green and wilted, about 2 minutes. Pour the spinach into a colander and apply pressure to the top with a towel to remove all of the liquid. Transfer the spinach to a cutting board and coarsely chop.

Drain the artichoke hearts and reserve the leaves from two hearts. Chop the rest of the hearts and add them to the cashew sauce along with the spinach and mayonnaise. Mix until combined. Place the dip in a 3-quart round baking dish and lay the reserved artichoke leaves on top. Bake for 20 minutes, or until bubbling on the sides and browned on top. Serve with the raw vegetables alongside.

make it ahead Prepare the dip up to 2 days in advance, wrap it tightly, and store in the refrigerator. Bring to room temperature before baking, about 1 hour.

tidbits For those who can tolerate dairy and want a more traditional cheesy dip, substitute 1 pound cream cheese and ½ cup sour cream for the cashews, apple cider vinegar, and lemon juice.

1 small shallot, peeled and quartered

4 cloves garlic

½-inch piece fresh ginger, peeled

1 stalk lemongrass, white part only, minced

2 pounds boneless, skinless chicken thighs, trimmed of visible fat and cut into chunks

2 tablespoons fish sauce

2 tablespoons tamarind paste

¼ cup chopped fresh cilantro, plus more for garnish

½ teaspoon fine sea salt

½ teaspoon freshly ground black pepper

40 small butter lettuce leaves, for serving

1 cucumber, chopped, for garnish

1 small red onion, chopped, for garnish

sauce

1 cup water

1 teaspoon arrowroot powder

½ cup white wine vinegar

½ cup coconut sugar

¼ cup light-colored raw honey

2 cloves garlic, minced

1½ tablespoons minced fresh red chile

2 teaspoons peeled and minced fresh ginger

2 teaspoons tamarind paste

2 teaspoons fish sauce

thai chicken meatballs with tamarind chile sauce

These meatballs are packed with bold Thai flavors, and the tangy chile sauce gives this delectable appetizer a little heat. While they may be bite-size, they are filling.

Preheat the oven to 400°F. Lightly grease a rimmed baking sheet.

Combine the shallot, garlic, ginger, and lemongrass in a food processor. Process until finely chopped. Add the chicken and process again until coarsely chopped. Add the fish sauce, tamarind, cilantro, salt, and pepper. Process once more until the chicken is minced and mixed well. Roll the mixture into 1-inch balls to make about 40 bite-size meatballs. Place the meatballs on the baking sheet and bake for 15 minutes, or until cooked through.

To make the sauce, combine ¼ cup of the water with the arrowroot powder and whisk together. Set aside.

Combine the remaining ¾ cup water, the vinegar, coconut sugar, honey, garlic, chile, ginger, tamarind paste, and fish sauce in a saucepan and bring to a boil. Reduce the heat to maintain a low boil and simmer for 15 minutes, or until the sauce reduces by about half. Whisk in the arrowroot mixture and simmer for an additional 5 minutes to thicken.

Serve the meatballs inside of the lettuce cups and top each with a drizzle of sauce and some cucumber, red onion, and cilantro.

make it ahead Make the meatballs up to 2 days in advance and store them raw in an airtight container in the refrigerator. The sauce can be stored in an airtight container in the refrigerator for up to 1 week. Reheat it in a saucepan over low heat while the meatballs are baking, adding a bit of water to thin it out if it becomes too thick.

tidbit Tamarind is a uniquely flavored fruit that lends a bright and slightly sour flavor you might recognize from a good *pad Thai*. Look for brands that are 100 percent fruit concentrate without the seeds or added ingredients. You can find tamarind paste in the Thai or Indian food section of your supermarket or purchase it online.

crab-stuffed mushrooms

Stuffed mushrooms are always a favorite of mine at parties. They have an air of sophistication, but they're really simple to make. Crab makes this version decadent and worthy of celebrating a new year. You can also make a vegetarian version by simply leaving out the crabmeat.

SERVES 10

4 tablespoons ghee (page 325), grass-fed unsalted butter, or extra-virgin olive oil

40 cremini or white button mushrooms

1 small yellow onion, coarsely chopped

2 cups crabmeat (about 1 pound), picked through for shells

¼ cup mayonnaise (page 328)

1 teaspoon freshly squeezed lemon juice

1 teaspoon fine sea salt

1 teaspoon dried oregano

½ teaspoon dried thyme

¼ cup almond meal or finely ground golden flaxseed, for sprinkling

¼ cup chopped fresh flat-leaf parsley, for garnish

Preheat the oven to 350°F. Lightly grease two 9 by 13-inch baking dishes or two rimmed baking sheets with 1 tablespoon of the ghee.

Remove the stems from the mushrooms and set aside. Gently hollow out some of the inside of the mushroom cap and set the caps aside. Combine the mushroom stems and trimmings and the onion in a food processor and pulse until finely chopped.

Melt the remaining 3 tablespoons ghee in a skillet over medium-high heat. Add the chopped mushrooms and onions and sauté until soft, 5 to 7 minutes. Set aside to cool for 10 minutes.

Combine the crab, mayonnaise, lemon juice, salt, oregano, and thyme in a bowl, then mix in the sautéed mushroom mixture.

Fill each mushroom cap with a heaping tablespoon of the mixture and gently push down to fill the caps. Sprinkle the tops with the almond meal.

Place the stuffed caps in the prepared dishes and bake for 15 to 18 minutes, until the filling is hot and the mushrooms are tender and browned. Transfer the mushrooms to a platter and serve warm garnished with the parsley.

tidbits If you're allergic to shellfish or when crab is not in season, swap cooked and crumbled mild Italian sausage for the crabmeat.

champagne chocolate strawberries

For a simple but sophisticated treat to cap off your swanky New Year's Eve fête, try this version of chocolate-dipped strawberries. The berries are infused overnight with Champagne and then coated with a homemade chocolate shell. You will need a candy thermometer to make the chocolate shell, so be sure to have one on hand.

SERVES 10

30 medium strawberries with stems (about 1 quart)

1 (750-ml) bottle Champagne, Prosecco, or any brut sparkling wine

6 ounces raw cacao butter, chopped

5 tablespoons pure maple syrup

⅔ cup plus 2 tablespoons natural cocoa powder

Pinch of fine sea salt

½ teaspoon pure vanilla extract

Place the strawberries in a large bowl and add the Champagne. Gently cover with a light plate or bowl to keep the strawberries submerged and place in the refrigerator to soak overnight.

Drain the strawberries and place them on a clean towel to dry thoroughly. Heat 2 inches of water in a saucepan over medium heat until just barely simmering. In a glass bowl that fits inside the saucepan without touching the simmering water, add the cacao butter and whisk constantly for about 15 minutes, until the cacao butter is fully melted and registers 105°F on a candy thermometer.

Turn off the heat and carefully remove the glass bowl from the saucepan. Adding one ingredient at a time, gently whisk in the maple syrup, cocoa powder, salt, and vanilla and whisk until just combined. Switch to a rubber spatula and gently stir until the mixture has cooled. The chocolate should be smooth and shiny and have a slightly thickened liquid consistency. Let the chocolate sit at room temperature for 20 minutes to thicken a bit more.

tidbits The temperature of the cacao butter is important in order to get a smooth chocolate that tempers properly. If you overheat it, leave it on the counter and continue stirring occasionally until the temperature reduces to 105°F before adding the remaining ingredients.

Line a baking sheet with parchment paper. Holding a strawberry by the stem, dip it into the chocolate and place it on the baking sheet. Repeat with the remaining strawberries, then place the baking sheet in the refrigerator for 10 minutes, until the chocolate has hardened slightly. Remove the berries from the refrigerator and repeat with a second layer of the chocolate coating. Place in the refrigerator again to harden for at least 2 hours. Arrange the strawberries on a platter and serve chilled.

make it ahead These can be made up to 3 days in advance. Wrap the baking sheet tightly with plastic wrap and store in the refrigerator.

holiday gimlet

With the addition of red wine to lend a beautiful and festive red color, this gimlet is anything but ordinary. While the distillation process removes most gluten from the gin, be sure to choose a wheat-free gin to be safe. Make these in batches to serve as a signature cocktail throughout the night, or make them to order. A standard cocktail shaker will make one batch of this drink and serve three or four people, depending on the size of the serving glasses.

SERVES 4

6 ounces gin

3 ounces unsweetened cranberry juice

4 ounces honey syrup (see Tidbits)

2 ounces freshly squeezed lime juice

2 ounces dry red wine

½ cup ice

Fresh cranberries, for garnish

Combine the gin, cranberry juice, honey syrup, lime juice, and red wine in a cocktail shaker with the ice. Shake vigorously and strain into 4 chilled coupes. Garnish with 3 fresh cranberries on a cocktail pick or toothpick.

make it ahead To serve this to a large crowd, combine 2¼ cups gin, 1¼ cups cold water, 1 cup plus 2 tablespoons cranberry juice, 1½ cups honey syrup, ¾ cup lime juice, and ¾ cup red wine in a large pitcher or punch bowl and stir to combine. Store the gimlet in the refrigerator for up to 24 hours, and add the cranberries for garnish just before serving.

If the punch will sit at room temperature for more than an hour, make a decorative ice mold to keep it cold. Fill a 9-inch round cake or Bundt pan with water, add fresh cranberries, and freeze. When ready to serve, add the ice mold to the punch bowl. (Using an ice mold rather than ice cubes prevents the punch from becoming diluted.)

tidbits I substitute honey syrup for simple syrup (white sugar and water) in cocktails. Take 1 part honey and dissolve it in 1 part hot, but not boiling, water. Use a light-colored honey, such as raw clover honey, so the flavor of the honey does not overpower the drink. Make 2 cups (16 ounces) at a time (using 1 cup honey and 1 cup boiling water) and store in a sealed bottle or container in the fridge for up to a month.

nye 75

A traditional French 75 uses gin and simple syrup, but my brother, Joel, made this celebratory variation using apple brandy and honey syrup. Apple brandy is a full-proof, barrel-aged spirit made from fermented and distilled apples, so it's perfect for gluten- and grain-free cocktails. Joel suggests using Laird's bonded 100-proof apple brandy here.

SERVES 4

4 ounces 100-proof apple brandy

4 ounces freshly squeezed lemon juice

3 ounces honey syrup (see Tidbits, page 43)

½ cup ice

12 ounces Champagne or other sparkling wine

Lemon peel, for garnish

Add the apple brandy, lemon juice, and honey syrup to a cocktail shaker with the ice. Shake vigorously and strain the beverage into 4 chilled champagne flutes or other stemmed glasses. Top each flute with Champagne and garnish with a lemon peel.

make it ahead To make this as a punch to serve 12, combine 1½ cups each apple brandy, lemon juice, and cold water with 1¼ cups honey syrup in a punch bowl or large pitcher and stir to mix well. Store in the refrigerator until you are ready to serve. Cut 1 lemon and 1 apple into slices and place the slices in a 9-inch round cake or Bundt pan. Fill the pan with water, then freeze to make a decorative ice mold. When ready to serve, add the ice mold and 1 (750ml bottle) Champagne to the punch bowl.

game day
buffet

Although I grew up in Colorado, I was born in the San Francisco Bay Area, so my family has always cheered for both the California and the Colorado teams. We either hosted or attended a big Super Bowl party every year, and I will never forget the year when the Broncos played the 49ers! I'll admit, I was usually the one who preferred to be in the kitchen preparing food and refilling empty snack bowls during the game, but I always popped out to watch the commercials and the halftime show, which still holds true today.

When I was younger, my favorite game-day noshes were those unhealthy but quintessential and delicious snacks like Buffalo wings, chili-cheese dip with tortilla chips, and mini meatballs or hot dogs in a sweet-and-sour tomato sauce. The chili-cheese dip would be impossible to re-create Paleo style since it pretty much came from a can, but the rest of my favorites were easy to redesign. I also came up with a few new tasty dishes to add to the classics, like tender pork carnitas served atop mini plantain tostadas and rich chocolate cookies baked to look like footballs and filled with fluffy vanilla buttercream.

I think the perfect game-day snack is one you can make in the morning and keep warm in a slow cooker on a buffet during the game so people can help themselves as they please. There's no need to have the oven or stove on, or worse, eat cold food that's been sitting out all afternoon. Three of the recipes that follow make use of this tip, so call your friends and neighbors and gather an arsenal of slow cookers the next time your team is playing. I like to keep the drinks simple and opt for bottles that can be kept cold in an ice bucket so people can help themselves. Grab some gluten-free beer, hard apple cider (2 Towns Ciderhouse is our favorite), and some kombucha.

Impress your guests with more than just your big-screen television and serve them this delicious, hearty meal that lasts through the fourth quarter or the ninth inning. With a spread like this, fans will leave happy regardless of whether their team loses or wins.

Play ball!

menu

❖❖❖

Sweet-and-Sour Meatballs

Buffalo Wings with Herb Ranch Dressing

Cauliflower Buffalo Bites

Carnitas on Tostones

Green Chile Chicken Soup

❖❖❖

Whoopie Pies

sweet-and-sour meatballs

The meatballs you are probably used to having on game days contain bread crumbs and include white sugar or high-fructose corn syrup in the sauce. This grain-free version uses almond meal or coconut flour to bind the meatballs and natural sweeteners to flavor the sauce. Keep the meatballs warm in a slow cooker throughout the day so your guests can enjoy them until the game ends.

SERVES 10

sauce

3 cups tomato puree

¾ cup unsweetened pineapple juice

⅓ cup light-colored raw honey

⅓ cup coconut aminos

¼ cup tomato paste

2 tablespoons apple cider vinegar

2 tablespoons Dijon mustard

1½ teaspoons fine sea salt

½ teaspoon ground ginger

½ teaspoon onion powder

meatballs

2 small sweet onions, quartered

2 eggs

¼ cup almond meal, or 2 tablespoons coconut flour

2 pounds ground beef, chicken, turkey, or pork

1 tablespoon cold-pressed sesame oil

1½ teaspoons ground ginger

2 teaspoons fine sea salt

Preheat the oven to 350°F.

Make the sauce first by combining the tomato puree, pineapple juice, honey, coconut aminos, tomato paste, vinegar, mustard, salt, ginger, and onion powder in a saucepan. Bring to a boil, then reduce the heat to medium-low and let simmer, uncovered, for 45 minutes, or until thickened.

Meanwhile, make the meatballs. Pulse the onion in a food processor until finely minced. Add the eggs, almond meal, beef, sesame oil, ginger, and salt and pulse until fully combined.

Roll the meat mixture into 3 dozen bite-size meatballs. Space the meatballs evenly on two rimmed baking sheets and bake for 12 minutes, turning the meatballs once halfway through, until browned and cooked through.

Once the sauce has thickened, transfer it and the meatballs to a slow cooker set to low. Cover until ready to serve.

make it ahead The sauce and meatballs can be cooked up to 3 days in advance. Store them separately so the pineapple enzymes don't break down the meat. The morning of the big game, combine them in a slow cooker and set it to low to reheat. To freeze ahead, cool the cooked meatballs and sauce separately in the refrigerator, then place each in an airtight container and freeze for up to 3 months. Thaw in the refrigerator overnight and reheat on the stove over medium-low heat, or place them in a slow cooker on low heat until heated through, about 2 hours.

tidbits If using poultry, select dark meat to keep these meatballs moist and flavorful.

buffalo wings with herb ranch dressing

These crispy and spicy Buffalo wings are free from heavy batters and breading and are delicious when dipped in a cool ranch dressing. Most traditional wings are served with blue cheese dressing, but for a dairy-free option, my herb ranch really satisfies the need for a tangy dip. If you also plan to make the Cauliflower Buffalo Bites (page 54), double the dressing recipe and serve it alongside both dishes.

SERVES 10

3 pounds whole chicken wings

⅓ cup melted ghee (page 325), grass-fed unsalted butter, or coconut oil

1½ teaspoons fine sea salt

1 teaspoon cayenne pepper

½ cup pepper sauce

2 teaspoons white wine vinegar

Herb ranch dressing (page 326), for serving

5 carrots, peeled and cut into sticks, for serving

5 ribs celery, cut into sticks, for serving

Preheat the oven to 400°F.

Allow the wings to sit at room temperature for 30 minutes. Remove the tips from the wings and reserve for chicken stock (page 327), if desired. Separate the wings at the joint. In a bowl, toss the wing parts with 3 tablespoons of the melted ghee, 1 teaspoon of the salt, and ½ teaspoon of the cayenne. Arrange the chicken on a wire rack set over a rimmed baking sheet. Bake for 35 to 40 minutes, until crisp, turning the wings over halfway through.

Meanwhile, prepare the wing sauce by combining the pepper sauce, the remaining 2½ tablespoons melted ghee, the vinegar, the remaining ½ teaspoon salt, and the remaining ½ teaspoon cayenne. Toss the wings in the sauce and serve immediately with the dressing and carrot and celery sticks on the side.

make it ahead To save on prep time, make the dressing and the wing sauce the day before the game and store them in airtight containers in the refrigerator. Reheat the sauce in a saucepan over low heat before tossing in the wings.

tidbits The type of pepper sauce you use is important. A lot of hot sauces have hidden ingredients and can contain gluten, so I love to use the Arizona Pepper's Jalapeño Pepper Sauce or a classic Frank's RedHot, which you can find at a lot of health food stores or online. A cayenne, habanero, or jalapeño sauce will work, but each has a different level of spiciness, so choose one that suits your taste. When checking the labels, look for simplicity: peppers, vinegar, and salt.

cauliflower buffalo bites

For a lighter, vegetarian take on the classic, game-day Buffalo wings, I used battered cauliflower as a stand-in for the wings. Once you pop one of these crispy bites of spice into your mouth, you won't be able to stop. Use coconut oil in place of the ghee to make these vegan.

SERVES 10

1 cup water

1 cup arrowroot powder

¼ cup coconut flour

2 teaspoons garlic powder

1½ teaspoons fine sea salt

½ teaspoon cayenne pepper

2 heads cauliflower, stems trimmed and cut into bite-size florets

sauce

¼ cup melted ghee (page 325), grass-fed unsalted butter, or coconut oil

½ cup pepper sauce

1½ teaspoons fine sea salt

2 teaspoons white wine vinegar

¾ teaspoon cayenne pepper

Herb ranch dressing (page 326), for serving

5 carrots, peeled and cut into sticks, for serving

5 ribs celery, cut into sticks, for serving

Preheat the oven to 450°F. Grease a wire rack with olive oil. Set the rack over a rimmed baking sheet.

In a bowl, whisk together the water, arrowroot powder, coconut flour, garlic powder, salt, and cayenne. Dip the cauliflower pieces in the batter, then place them on the prepared wire rack. Bake for 10 minutes, flip, then bake for an additional 10 minutes, or until browned and crisp.

To make the sauce, in a bowl, whisk together the melted ghee, pepper sauce, salt, vinegar, and cayenne pepper. Toss the cauliflower bites in the sauce and shake off any excess liquid. Return the cauliflower pieces to the wire rack and bake for 5 minutes more. Serve immediately with the dressing and carrot and celery sticks on the side.

make it ahead To save on prep time, make up the dressing and the sauce 3 days before the game and store them in airtight containers in the refrigerator. Gently reheat the sauce in a saucepan over low heat before tossing in the cauliflower.

tidbits The type of sauce you use is important for both flavor and ingredients (see Tidbits, page 53).

carnitas on tostones

A flavorful pork roast is cooked to perfection in a slow cooker, then served on top of *tostones*, or twice-fried plantains, and topped with tangy pickled onions, avocado, and cilantro. Leave the slow cooker on low heat throughout the game so fans can help themselves during commercials and halftime.

SERVES 10

4 cloves garlic, minced

2½ teaspoons fine sea salt, plus more to sprinkle

1 teaspoon ground cumin

1 teaspoon dried oregano

¼ teaspoon ground cinnamon

1 (4-pound) boneless pork shoulder roast, trimmed of fat

1 cup chicken stock (page 327)

1 small yellow onion, halved and thinly sliced lengthwise

1 to 3 dried chipotle chiles, seeded and finely chopped

2 bay leaves

Pickled onions (page 329), for serving

½ cup fresh cilantro leaves, for serving

3 avocados, pitted, peeled, and diced, for serving

tostones

4 green (unripe) plantains

Coconut oil, ghee (page 325), or palm shortening, for frying

Fine sea salt

Mix together the garlic, salt, cumin, oregano, and cinnamon. Rub the mixture all over the pork roast. Pour the chicken stock into a 6-quart slow cooker and add the onion, chipotles, and bay leaves. Place the meat on top, then cover and cook for 8 hours on low. Remove the roast and the bay leaves from the slow cooker and shred the meat using two forks. Return the shredded meat to the slow cooker and stir to combine with the juices.

To make the tostones, peel the plantains and cut them into 2-inch-long pieces. Heat 2 inches of oil in a skillet over medium-high heat until the oil reaches 375°F. Fry the pieces on all sides until lightly golden, about 2 minutes. Transfer the plantains to a cutting board with a slotted spoon and smash each piece using a flat spatula or the bottom of a glass to create a flat disk about ¼ inch thick. Return the disks to the hot oil and fry for a second time for 1 to 2 minutes, until browned and crisp. Remove from the oil to a plate lined with paper towels and lightly sprinkle with salt.

Transfer the tostones to a serving platter and set them out alongside the pork and pickled onions, cilantro, and avocado. Let your guests use tongs or a slotted spoon to top their tostones with the shredded pork and toppings of their choice.

make it ahead The meat can be cooked up to 3 days in advance and reheated on the stove top or in a slow cooker. To freeze, place all of the uncooked contents of the slow cooker in an airtight container and freeze for up to 6 months. Defrost in the refrigerator overnight, then cook as directed. Tostones are best served immediately after frying, but can be arranged in a single layer on a baking sheet and kept in a warm oven until ready to serve.

tidbits Unripe plantains can be found in many health food stores near the bananas, or at Asian markets. If you are unable to locate them, substitute waffle-cut sweet potato fries, individual pizza crusts (see page 72), or lettuce cups.

green chile chicken soup

A soup bar is perfect for game-day meals. Keep the soup warm in the slow cooker straight through to the fourth quarter; guests can customize their own bowls with toppings served on the side.

SERVES 10

3 pounds bone-in, skinless chicken thighs, trimmed of fat

5 cups chicken stock (page 327)

2 (4-ounce) cans fire-roasted green chiles and their juices

1 yellow onion, diced

1 green (unripe) plantain, peeled and diced

1 parsnip, peeled and diced

1 jalapeño chile, seeded and diced

3 cloves garlic, minced

1 tablespoon fine sea salt

1 tablespoon ground cumin

1 teaspoon ground coriander

1 teaspoon ground white pepper

2 cups plantain chips, for serving

4 avocados, pitted, peeled, and sliced, for serving

1 cup torn fresh cilantro leaves, for serving

3 limes, cut into wedges, for serving

Put the chicken thighs in a 6-quart slow cooker. Add the chicken stock, green chiles, onion, plantain, parsnip, jalapeño, garlic, salt, cumin, coriander, and white pepper. Cover and cook for 6 hours on low. Remove the chicken and shred it from the bone. Return the meat to the slow cooker and stir to combine.

Serve the soup in the slow cooker on the warm setting. Place the slow cooker on the buffet table and set bowls and spoons next to it. Put the plantain chips, avocados, cilantro, and lime wedges in small separate bowls and place alongside, so guests can help themselves.

make it ahead Put all of the ingredients into the slow cooker insert the night before and store it, covered, in the refrigerator. Put the insert into the slow cooker the morning of the big game, turn it on, and forget it!

To freeze, combine all of the ingredients except the serving ingredients in an airtight container and place in the freezer for up to 6 months. Defrost in the refrigerator overnight, then cook in the slow cooker as directed.

whoopie pies

Every game-day party needs a sweet, fudgy treat at the end to celebrate the big win, or console a loss! These football-shaped dark chocolate cookies with vanilla buttercream filling are sure to serve either cause. I use Dutch-processed cocoa here to give the cookies a dark chocolate color and rich flavor.

MAKES 10 PIES

⅓ cup palm shortening

½ cup coconut sugar

2 tablespoons light-colored raw honey

2 eggs, at room temperature

1 teaspoon pure vanilla extract

1 teaspoon freshly squeezed lemon juice

2 tablespoons arrowroot powder

½ cup Dutch-processed cocoa powder

½ cup coconut flour

½ teaspoon grain-free baking powder (page 325)

½ teaspoon baking soda

¼ teaspoon fine sea salt

¾ cup full-fat coconut milk

2 cups Vanilla Buttercream (page 160)

Preheat the oven to 350°F. Cut two sheets of parchment paper to fit two rimmed baking sheets. Using a pencil, trace 10 football shapes each 1½ inches in diameter on each sheet, spacing them evenly. Turn the sheets over and place on the pans.

To make the cookies, in the bowl of a stand mixer fitted with the beater attachment, or using an electric handheld beater, cream together the palm shortening, coconut sugar, and honey for 1 minute on medium-high speed. Add the eggs, vanilla, and lemon juice and beat again until combined. Combine the arrowroot, cocoa powder, coconut flour, baking powder, baking soda, and salt in a bowl. Slowly beat in the flour mixture, alternating with the coconut milk, until blended.

Using a cookie scoop, drop the batter onto the prepared baking sheets. Using a toothpick or an offset spatula, gently draw the batter out to fill in the traced shapes. Alternatively, pipe the batter to fill the traced shapes.

Bake for 15 to 18 minutes, until the cookies are slightly crisp on the outside. Cool completely on a wire rack.

To assemble, fill a piping bag fitted with a plain tip with the buttercream. Turn one cookie over so the bottom is facing up. Starting from the perimeter, pipe the buttercream onto the bottom, covering it completely. Gently press the bottom side of another cookie on top. Repeat to make 10 filled cookies. Use the remaining buttercream to pipe football laces onto the top of each whoopie pie.

make it ahead The pies can be baked and assembled up to 3 days in advance. Wrap tightly and store in the refrigerator until you are ready to serve. The cookies can also be baked and frozen in a single layer on a baking sheet lined with parchment paper, then wrapped individually and stored for up to 6 months. Defrost in the refrigerator overnight prior to filling with frosting.

valentine's day

a little love for the kids

I vividly remember waking up every morning on Valentine's Day to a special breakfast prepared by my mom. She usually made us an egg-in-a-hole, with the toast cutout shaped like a heart. The table was always set with heart confetti scattered about, and each of us kids would have a big chocolate heart at our place setting.

I've continued this cherished tradition with my own family by surprising my kids with an entire day of love. We start with a beet-red nutritious smoothie or a special breakfast of pancakes and strawberries threaded onto "Cupid's arrows." Asher loves to help make the heart-shaped snacks for his lunch box, and I usually slip in a little love note. For dinner, we make individual pizzas and everyone gets to pick toppings that we cut into mini heart shapes. When Valentine's Day starts to approach, Asher inevitably starts asking about all of his heart-shaped surprises to come.

Happy love day!

my heart beets for you smoothie

Beets and berries combine to produce a vibrant magenta hue, creating a festive and nutritious start to your little ones' day of love. We are always rushed in the morning to get our oldest son, Asher, off to school, so I frequently send him with a smoothie to drink in the car. This is one of his favorites.

MAKES 4 (6-OUNCE)
SMOOTHIES

1 cup almond milk
(page 320)

1 tart apple, cored and
quartered

1 cup frozen strawberries,
about 8 whole berries

¾ cup frozen raspberries

1 frozen banana, cut into
pieces

½ cup peeled and diced raw
or cooked beets (see Tidbits)

1 tablespoon freshly
squeezed lemon juice

Pour the almond milk into the blender. Add the apple, strawberries, raspberries, banana, beets, and lemon juice and blend on low for 30 seconds, then high for 30 seconds until smooth. Pour into 4 glasses and serve immediately.

tidbits I like to use roasted beets in this because the flavor is milder and thus more palatable for my son, but raw will work as well if you are using a high-speed blender. Look for cooked and peeled, ready-to-eat baby beets in the produce section, or roast a few beets and keep them in the refrigerator for up to 3 days.

cupid's arrow pancakes

These fluffy heart-shaped pancake skewers are sure to win the hearts of your little ones, plus they are fun for dipping. Pick up lollipop sticks at any craft or party store, or use bamboo meat skewers cut in half.

SERVES 4

3 eggs

½ cup almond milk
(page 320)

2 tablespoons melted
coconut oil or ghee
(page 325)

¾ cup cashew flour

3 tablespoons coconut flour

2 tablespoons coconut
sugar or light-colored
raw honey

2 teaspoons arrowroot
powder

¾ teaspoon baking soda

½ teaspoon cream of tartar

⅛ teaspoon fine sea salt

1 cup strawberries, hulled
and halved

1 banana, sliced

Pure maple syrup,
for serving

Combine the eggs, almond milk, coconut oil, cashew flour, coconut flour, coconut sugar, arrowroot powder, baking soda, cream of tartar, and salt in a blender. Blend on low for 15 seconds. Let the batter sit for 5 minutes, then blend again on high for 15 seconds.

Lightly grease a griddle or a large skillet with palm shortening and set it over medium-high heat.

Using a piping bag fitted with a plain tip, pipe the batter into 2-inch heart shapes onto the hot pan. Cook for 2 minutes, or until bubbles appear on the surface and the edges release easily. Flip and continue cooking for 2 to 3 minutes, until cooked through. Alternatively, make standard circular-shaped pancakes and use a cookie cutter to cut out heart shapes after cooking. Repeat until all the pancake batter is used.

Thread the pancakes and fruits onto lollipop sticks in the following order: pancake, strawberry, banana, and pancake. Serve with a side of maple syrup.

make it ahead These pancakes freeze well, so make a double batch, store the pancakes in a resealable bag, and reheat them as needed in a toaster, the oven, or a skillet set over medium heat.

tidbits Substitute blanched almond flour, if desired, for the cashew flour. For nut-free pancakes, use finely ground sunflower seeds (see page 19), add ½ teaspoon freshly squeezed lemon juice to the batter, and reduce the baking soda by half.

Palm shortening works best to grease the pan and will create the lightest colored pancakes. Grain-free pancakes take a bit longer to cook than traditional ones, so make sure the first side is completely cooked before trying to flip.

Happy
Love Day!
♡Mom

lunch box love

Send your child to school with a lunch box full of love to keep him or her feeling special all day long. This is more of an idea than a recipe, so feel free to have fun with it and be inspired. Leftover Be Mine Pizza (page 72) also makes a great school lunch.

SERVES 1

grain-free pinwheels

Fill my grain-free wraps (page 326) with the fillings of your choice, roll them up tightly, and slice them into 1-inch pieces. Here are some possible filling ideas:

- Ham, mayonnaise, and sliced tomatoes

- Red raspberry jam with sunflower seed butter

- Whipped cream (page 332), sliced strawberries, sliced bananas, and a sprinkle of cinnamon

- Cashew cream (page 324) or herb ranch dressing (page 326) with thinly sliced smoked salmon and thinly sliced cucumber strips

- Store-bought beet hummus with thinly sliced radishes and thinly shaved carrot strips

veggie snacks

- Thinly slice red bell peppers, cucumbers, and carrots and then cut the pieces with a mini heart-shaped cookie cutter.

apple sunbutter sandwiches

Stand an apple upright and cut an even number of thin slices, avoiding the core. Use a heart-shaped cookie cutter to cut a heart in the center of half of the slices. Rub the apple slices all over with a little lemon juice to keep them from oxidizing. Spread the bottom slices (the ones without the heart cutouts) with sunflower seed butter, then sandwich the heart slices on top. Fill the heart shape by pressing mini chocolate chips, raisins, or raspberry jam into the exposed sunbutter.

be mine pizza

I wanted to make a pizza crust that nut- and egg-free kiddos could enjoy, so I created this version, which uses tahini, or sesame seed butter, in the dough where I would typically use almond butter, and chia and flaxseeds in place of the eggs. We always love to have pizza night when we all get to choose our own toppings. In addition to the classic pepperoni, ham and pineapple—which we cut into heart shapes to go with the theme—is a favorite topping at our house. Enjoy the pizza at home or pack it in a lunch box for a delicious nut-free school lunch. Of course, the crust is versatile and can also be used throughout the year.

SERVES 4

2 tablespoons finely ground white chia seeds

½ cup hot water

½ cup raw tahini

½ cup finely ground golden flaxseed

⅓ cup arrowroot powder

½ teaspoon garlic powder

½ teaspoon fine sea salt

1 teaspoon baking soda

2 teaspoons extra-virgin olive oil

Toppings: marinara sauce; heart-shaped sliced pepperoni; shredded mozzarella, Parmesan, or dairy-free cheese; fresh torn basil leaves

Preheat the oven to 400°F. Line two baking sheets with parchment paper.

Whisk together the chia seeds and water. Set aside to thicken for 5 minutes.

Mix the tahini very well, ensuring all of the oil is incorporated with the thick butter at the bottom of the jar. In a stand mixer fitted with the beater attachment, or using an electric handheld beater, combine the tahini, flaxseed, arrowroot, garlic powder, salt, and baking soda on medium speed. Add the thickened chia slurry and beat on high speed for 30 seconds, or until well incorporated.

Split the dough in half and turn it out onto the prepared baking sheets. Using slightly wet fingers, press the dough into two 9-inch circles or heart shapes about ⅛ inch thick. Brush the tops with the olive oil.

Bake for 15 minutes, or until golden. Add the desired toppings and continue baking for 5 minutes, or until the toppings are heated through. Slice into wedges and serve immediately.

make it ahead Baked pizza crusts can be tightly wrapped in plastic wrap and frozen for 6 months. Heat the frozen crust in a 400°F oven for 15 minutes prior to topping.

tidbits If black chia seeds and brown flaxseeds are used, the color of the pizza will change significantly, but the flavor and texture will remain the same.

Look for nitrate-free and sugar-free pepperoni, or replace the pepperoni with whatever your little Valentine's heart desires: ham, chicken, or sausage. If your little one is dairy-free, try a nut-based cheese substitute like Kite Hill brand or add 2 teaspoons nutritional yeast to the dough for a cheese-like flavor.

dinner for two

For the adults, a more sophisticated meal is in order, but with an equal amount of love put into the preparation. My birthday falls close to Valentine's Day, so Ryan and I have been combining the two occasions since we started dating in high school. We rarely exchange gifts for Valentine's Day anymore, and we choose to stay in to avoid overcrowded and overpriced restaurant dinners featuring mediocre food.

My gift to Ryan is usually a homemade meal featuring his favorite foods: an iceberg wedge salad reminiscent of the steak-house favorite, slow-cooked short ribs braised in red wine, and rapini cooked with garlic and a little spice. He ends up joining me in the kitchen after the kids go to bed, but only to grab some bacon off the plate before I put it on the salad! I always have a bottle of Cabernet to enjoy over dinner, but you could also make the Holiday Gimlet (page 43) for a festive red cocktail. We finish the night with two of our favorites things: caramel and chocolate.

Even though this dinner is designed for two, it takes a lot of work to prepare such a feast, so I scaled the dishes to serve four. That makes it work for a double date or a night in with some friends. The ribs are even better the second day, and the rest of the dishes hold well, so you can also go ahead and make this on the thirteenth, enjoy it on the fourteenth, and then reap the labors of your love a second time with leftovers on the fifteenth! They say the way to a man's heart is through his stomach, and this meal is sure to leave a lasting impression.

Happy Valentine's Day!

wedge salad with herb ranch dressing

Iceberg lettuce surely doesn't provide a lot of nutrients, and this may be the simplest of salads, but a crisp wedge with creamy dressing, crispy bacon, and lots of vegetables is Ryan's favorite steak-house salad. Blue cheese dressing typically accompanies this classic dish, but it contains dairy and often wheat from the cheese, so I use my dairy-free herb ranch dressing here. See my note below about how to transform this dressing into a creamy blue cheese version, if you are not keeping dairy-free.

SERVES 4

4 red baby beets

4 slices thick-cut bacon

1 head iceberg lettuce, cut into 4 wedges

½ cup cherry tomatoes, halved

2 carrots, peeled and shaved into thin ribbons

2 small radishes, thinly sliced

½ cup herb ranch dressing (page 326)

Preheat the oven to 400°F.

Place the beets in an oven-safe dish and cover tightly with aluminum foil. Bake for 45 minutes, or until the beets are tender. Remove from the oven and set aside until the beets are cool enough to handle; leave the oven on. Rub off the skins with a towel and cut the beets into halves, or quarters if they are on the larger side. Put the bacon on a rimmed baking sheet and bake for 12 to 15 minutes, until the bacon is crispy. Transfer the bacon to a plate lined with a paper towel to drain and cool, then chop the slices into bite-size pieces.

Assemble the salads by placing a wedge on each plate and topping with the roasted beets, bacon, tomatoes, carrots, radishes, and a drizzle of dressing. Serve immediately with any additional dressing on the side.

make it ahead Roast the beets, cook the bacon, and cut up the carrots and radishes up to 2 days in advance. Store the bacon and beets together in the refrigerator in an airtight container, and store the carrots and radishes together submerged in a bowl of water and tightly covered. Wash and quarter the lettuce, wrap it in a damp paper towel, and store in a bag in the refrigerator for up to 2 days. The salads can be plated without the dressing a few hours in advance and stored in the refrigerator. Drizzle on the dressing just before serving.

tidbits To turn the herb ranch dressing into a blue cheese dressing, omit the parsley, chives, and dill and stir in ¼ cup crumbled blue cheese. Use Humboldt Fog goat's milk cheese to get blue cheese flavor in a gluten-free and cow's milk–free cheese.

4 pounds bone-in beef short ribs, cut crosswise into 4-inch pieces

Fine sea salt and freshly ground black pepper

2 tablespoons chopped fresh thyme

2 tablespoons chopped fresh rosemary

2 tablespoons extra-virgin olive oil, ghee (page 325), or bacon fat

2 carrots, peeled and sliced into thick rounds

2 ribs celery, cut into thick slices

½ cup chopped leeks, white and tender green parts

3 cloves garlic, minced

1 (750-ml) bottle Cabernet Sauvignon

2 cups beef stock, homemade (page 327) or any store-bought low-sodium beef broth

2 tablespoons tomato paste

1 bay leaf

Chopped fresh flat-leaf parsley, for garnish

puree

8 ounces parsnips, peeled and cubed

4 ounces turnips, peeled and cubed

¼ cup chicken stock (page 327)

2 tablespoons ghee (page 325) or grass-fed unsalted butter

½ teaspoon fine sea salt

¼ teaspoon freshly ground black pepper

cabernet-braised short ribs with parsnip-turnip puree

My husband, Ryan, has a special affinity for braised meats that fall off the bone. I have been making variations of short ribs for years, which is why a different recipe appears in each of my three cookbooks. These short ribs are braised in wine and will melt in your mouth.

***

Arrange the ribs in a nonreactive dish and season each side generously with salt, pepper, thyme, and rosemary. Cover and refrigerate overnight. Let the meat sit at room temperature for 1 hour before cooking. Preheat the oven to 350°F and set the rack on the bottom rung.

Coat a large Dutch oven or wide ovenproof pot with olive oil and set over medium-high heat. Working in batches, add the ribs to the pot and cook each side for 2 to 3 minutes, until browned all over. Remove the ribs with tongs and set aside. Add the carrots, celery, leeks, and garlic and sauté for 5 minutes, or until the leeks are browned and fragrant. Stir in the wine, scraping up the browned bits off the bottom of the pot. Add the stock, tomato paste, and bay leaf. Return the ribs to the pot and bring to a boil.

Cover and braise for 2 hours, turning the ribs halfway through. Uncover and cook for 45 minutes more to reduce the sauce. Test the doneness by dragging a fork along the meat. If it shreds easily, or the bones fall out, they are done. Skim off any fat and season with salt and pepper to taste.

To make the puree, fill a pot with cold water and add the parsnips and turnips. Bring to a boil, partially cover, and cook for 15 minutes, or until fork-tender. Drain the vegetables and transfer to a food processor. Add the stock, ghee, salt, and pepper and puree until smooth. Cover and keep warm until the meat is finished cooking. If necessary, reheat in the hot oven 15 minutes prior to the ribs finishing. Serve the short ribs over the puree and top with a spoonful of pan juices and fresh parsley.

make it ahead The ribs can be made the day before. Cover and reheat in a 350°F oven for 30 minutes, or until heated through. Prepare the puree up to 3 days in advance and reheat it in a covered oven-safe dish at 350°F for 30 minutes.

tidbits Don't buy cheap wine for cooking. It should be smooth and tasty.

chile garlic rapini

Rapini, or broccoli rabe, is an earthy and nutty winter vegetable, and both the leaves and the buds are edible. I love to sauté it with some garlic, red pepper flakes, and a little acid to balance out the slightly bitter taste of the vegetable.

SERVES 4

2 teaspoons extra-virgin olive oil or ghee (page 325)

1 clove garlic, thinly sliced

1 pound rapini, ends trimmed

⅛ teaspoon dried red pepper flakes

Fine sea salt and freshly ground black pepper

1 teaspoon freshly squeezed lemon juice

2 teaspoons water

Heat the oil in a skillet over medium-high heat, add the garlic, and sauté for 30 seconds, or until golden and fragrant. Transfer to a plate. Add the rapini and red pepper flakes and season with salt and pepper. Cook, stirring occasionally, for 3 minutes. Add the lemon juice and water, cover, and cook for an additional 2 minutes, or until bright green and just tender. Return the garlic to the pan and serve hot.

tidbits Broccolini, mustard greens, or even standard broccoli can be substituted here.

salted caramel–chocolate panna cotta

Nothing says romance like caramel and dark chocolate. With a rich chocolate bottom, an airy caramel pudding-like center, and crispy spiced nuts on top, this dessert is a labor of love, but worth the effort.

chocolate ganache

2.5 ounces unsweetened baking chocolate, chopped

6 tablespoons full-fat coconut milk

2 tablespoons pure maple syrup

salted caramel

½ cup coconut sugar

1 tablespoon water

½ teaspoon fine sea salt

¼ cup full-fat coconut milk

panna cotta

1 cup almond milk (page 320)

2¼ teaspoons unflavored gelatin powder

1 cup full-fat coconut milk

½ vanilla bean, halved lengthwise and seeds scraped

spiced candied pecans

¼ cup pecans, coarsely chopped

1 tablespoon pure maple syrup

Pinch of cayenne pepper

Pinch of fine sea salt

Preheat the oven to 350°F. Line a baking sheet with parchment paper.

To make the ganache, combine the chocolate, coconut milk, and maple syrup in a glass bowl set over a saucepan with 2 inches of water in it, creating a double boiler. Bring the water to a boil and whisk until the chocolate has melted and the mixture is smooth. Divide the chocolate mixture evenly among 4 (16-ounce) glasses and place them in the refrigerator to set while you make the caramel and panna cotta.

To make the salted caramel, in a small saucepan, whisk together the coconut sugar, water, and salt and place over medium-high heat. Simmer for 5 to 7 minutes, until the mixture turns a dark amber color and a candy thermometer reads 240°F. Remove from the heat and immediately whisk in the coconut milk. Set aside to cool.

To make the panna cotta, pour ½ cup of the almond milk into a bowl and sprinkle the gelatin over the top. Let it sit for 5 minutes to bloom. Meanwhile, heat the remaining ½ cup almond milk, coconut milk, and vanilla bean seeds and pod in a saucepan over medium-high heat until barely simmering. Take the saucepan off the heat and whisk in the gelatin mixture until fully dissolved. Whisk in the salted caramel mixture until fully incorporated. Set aside to cool for 10 minutes.

To make the spiced candied pecans, in a bowl, combine the pecans, maple syrup, cayenne, and salt. Pour the mixture onto the prepared baking sheet and bake for 15 minutes. Remove from the oven and let cool.

Remove the glasses from the fridge and divide the salted caramel panna cotta mixture evenly over the cooled chocolate. Cover the glasses with plastic wrap pressed directly onto the panna cotta and refrigerate for 6 hours to set. Serve with the spiced candied pecans sprinkled on top.

make it ahead Make this dessert up to 5 days in advance and store in the refrigerator. Store the cooled nuts at room temperature in a sealed airtight container and sprinkle on top right before serving.

easter
brunch

menu

◆◆◆

Caramel-Pecan Sticky Buns

Asparagus Prosciutto Tart

*Butter Lettuce, Citrus,
and Haricots Verts Salad*

*Lavender-Rosemary
Leg of Lamb*

*Blood Orange and Honey—
Glazed Ham*

Sweet Potato Orange Cups

◆◆◆

Carrot Cake

◆◆◆

Lavender Lemonade

One of my family's Easter traditions involves a big brunch at a local hotel or our favorite restaurant. It is typically a buffet full of glorious springtime foods, which I love because I am completely indecisive when it comes to ordering. I try a little of this and a little of that, and I also have a hard time deciding whether to order breakfast or lunch. A brunch buffet is the perfect solution for me. I can have a little ham and a little lamb, a bit of fruit, an egg dish, and a sweet treat. There's nothing better than variety, especially when there's lots of celebratory foods that you typically only get once a year.

With that buffet concept in mind, I wrote this menu with multiple options. Choose either a sweet and tangy orange-honey baked ham or a succulent leg of lamb doused in lavender and rosemary and roasted to perfection. For breakfast lovers, line the buffet with gooey caramel sticky buns and a vibrant baked egg and spring vegetable tart.

These recipes work well for Easter, or you can modify them a bit for a Passover gathering. Mix and match them with the recipes in the next chapter for a special Mother's Day brunch, or just serve them on a lovely spring day when the weather has finally turned warm enough to dine outside.

Happy Easter!

caramel-pecan sticky buns

My grandma Bonnie always used to buy a cinnamon coffee cake for our Easter celebration, so I love to make these cinnamon-filled sticky buns in her memory.

dough

3¾ cups blanched almond flour

½ cup plus 2 tablespoons arrowroot powder

¼ cup plus 2 tablespoons coconut flour

3 eggs

3 tablespoons coconut sugar

3 tablespoons cold water

1 tablespoon grain-free baking powder (page 325)

¼ cup palm shortening or grass-fed unsalted butter, softened

½ teaspoons apple cider vinegar

filling

2 tablespoons melted ghee (page 325), grass-fed unsalted butter, or coconut oil

¼ cup coconut sugar

⅓ cup light-colored raw honey

3 tablespoons chopped raisins

1 tablespoon ground cinnamon

topping

1 cup coconut sugar

3 tablespoons ghee (page 325), coconut oil, or grass-fed unsalted butter

½ cup full-fat coconut milk

3 tablespoons light-colored raw honey

3 teaspoons arrowroot powder

¼ teaspoon fine sea salt

½ cup pecans, coarsely chopped

To make the dough, combine the almond flour, arrowroot, and coconut flour in a food processor and process for 15 seconds. Add the eggs, coconut sugar, water, and baking powder and pulse a few times until fully incorporated. Add the shortening and vinegar and process until the dough sticks together. Gather the dough into a ball, then flatten it into a disk and wrap tightly. Refrigerate for 30 minutes.

To make the filling, mix together the ghee, coconut sugar, honey, raisins, and cinnamon in a small bowl and set aside.

To make the topping, stir together the coconut sugar, ghee, coconut milk, honey, arrowroot, and salt in a saucepan over medium heat. Bring to a boil, then reduce the heat and simmer for 15 minutes. Set aside off the heat.

Preheat the oven to 350°F. Very lightly grease a 9-inch pie pan. Roll out the dough between two pieces of parchment paper into a ½-inch-thick oval. Spread the filling evenly over the dough, then roll up the dough tightly, like a jelly roll. Gently seal the seam with your fingers. Using a serrated knife, slice the log into ten 1½-inch pieces.

Pour half of the topping mixture into the bottom of the prepared pan and sprinkle the pecans over all. Transfer the buns, cut sides up, to the pan and nestle them together closely. Bake for 35 minutes, until the buns are golden on top. Remove from the oven and pour the remaining topping mixture over the top. Cool for 15 minutes, then invert the pan onto a platter to release the buns. Serve warm.

make it ahead Fill and roll the dough up to 2 days in advance. Wrap it tightly and refrigerate. Slice right before baking. The topping mixture can be stored in an airtight container in the refrigerator for up to 3 days. Gently rewarm before using. To freeze, slightly underbake the buns and cool to room temperature before wrapping tightly and storing in the freezer for up to 6 months. Defrost overnight in the refrigerator, then place the dish in a 350°F oven until warmed through, about 15 minutes.

asparagus prosciutto tart

Breakfast tarts are elegant and tasty and can be served for breakfast, lunch, or in between. This tart is not only a treat for the eyes but is also full of beautiful spring vegetables and rich flavors from the egg yolks and prosciutto.

SERVES 8

crust

3 cups blanched almond flour

1 egg

¼ cup arrowroot powder

2 tablespoons melted coconut oil

2 tablespoons cold water

½ teaspoon fine sea salt

filling

3 tablespoons extra-virgin olive oil

1 pound asparagus, trimmed and cut diagonally into ½-inch pieces

Juice from 1 lemon

2 cloves garlic, minced

⅓ cup cashew cream (page 324)

6 eggs

½ teaspoon fine sea salt

¼ teaspoon freshly ground black pepper

6 ounces thinly sliced prosciutto, cut into ribbons

1 cup microgreens

3 tablespoons chopped fresh chives

Preheat the oven to 325°F. Lightly grease an 11 by 7-inch tart pan.

To make the crust, combine the almond flour, egg, arrowroot, coconut oil, water, and salt in a stand mixer fitted with the beater attachment, or use an electric handheld mixer. Beat on medium speed until a loose dough forms. Gather the dough and press it into the bottom and up the sides of the tart pan. Bake for 15 minutes, or until the crust is golden on the edges. Remove the crust from the oven and increase the temperature to 375°F.

To make the filling, heat 1 tablespoon of the olive oil in a skillet over medium-high heat. Add the asparagus and ½ teaspoon of the lemon juice and sauté for 3 minutes. Add the garlic and continue cooking for 2 minutes, or until the asparagus is crisp-tender.

Spread the cashew cream on the bottom of the crust, then spoon in the asparagus mixture. Gently crack the eggs on top, spacing them out evenly. Sprinkle with the salt and pepper. Bake for 10 to 12 minutes, just until the egg whites are set and the yolks are still soft.

Remove from the oven and sprinkle with the prosciutto, microgreens, and chives. Drizzle with the remaining 2 tablespoons olive oil and the remaining lemon juice. Serve immediately.

make it ahead Bake the crust and make the cashew cream the day before to save time during your party preparations. Store the crust tightly wrapped and the cashew cream in an airtight container in the refrigerator. Bring them out to sit at room temperature while you prepare the filling.

tidbits To make this suitable for Passover, substitute smoked salmon for the prosciutto.

If you tolerate dairy, substitute crème fraîche for the cashew cream.

butter lettuce, citrus, and haricots verts salad

I just love how the burst of citrus in this salad balances the subtle licorice flavor from the fennel and the spice from the radish. I grew up eating jarred green mint jelly served over lamb at Easter time, so I took that familiar flavor and made a mint-shallot vinaigrette to toss with tender butter lettuce and crisp, thin green beans.

SERVES 8

8 ounces haricots verts (thin green beans), trimmed and halved

2 heads butter lettuce, leaves torn into bite-size pieces

6 radishes, thinly sliced

1 small fennel bulb, trimmed and shaved, a few fronds reserved for garnish

1 orange, peeled and segmented

1 small grapefruit, peeled and segmented

mint shallot vinaigrette

1 small clove garlic, minced

2 tablespoons minced shallot

1½ tablespoons champagne vinegar

1 tablespoon Dijon mustard

1 tablespoon freshly squeezed lemon juice

½ cup extra-virgin olive oil

Fine sea salt and freshly ground black pepper

1 tablespoon minced fresh mint leaves

Bring a large pot of water to a boil and add the haricot verts. Blanch for 5 minutes, drain, and transfer them to an ice bath until cooled.

Mix the lettuce, radishes, fennel, orange, and grapefruit in a large bowl. Add the beans once they have cooled.

To make the vinaigrette, whisk together the garlic, shallot, vinegar, mustard, and lemon juice. While whisking, slowly drizzle the olive oil into the bowl in a steady stream. Season with salt, pepper, and mint.

Toss the salad with ¼ cup of the dressing and serve immediately with fennel fronds to garnish and additional dressing on the side.

make it ahead Store the dressing in an airtight container in the refrigerator for up to 1 week. Prepare the salad ingredients up to 2 days in advance. Store the cut fennel, radishes, and blanched green beans in a bowl of water, tightly covered, in the refrigerator. Wash and dry the lettuce and wrap it in a damp paper towel in a bag in the fridge. Store the cut citrus in their juices in an airtight container in the refrigerator. Assemble and dress the salad prior to serving.

lavender-rosemary leg of lamb

I don't cook lamb that often, but Easter is one of the few special times during the year when we enjoy it. This leg of lamb has a beautiful bouquet of lavender and rosemary and can be served with a fragrant spiced shallot jam. My favorite part though, is the crispy browned sweet potatoes and parsnips that have cooked slowly in the juices of the lamb.

SERVES 8 TO 10

1 (6- to 7-pound) bone-in leg of lamb

½ cup extra-virgin olive oil

3 cloves garlic, peeled

3 tablespoons freshly squeezed lemon juice

3 sprigs rosemary, needles stripped from stem

2 tablespoons dried lavender

Fine sea salt and freshly ground black pepper

2 pounds sweet potatoes, scrubbed but not peeled and cut into wedges

2 pounds parsnips, peeled and cut into wedges

Moroccan spiced jam (page 329), for serving (optional)

Preheat the oven to 450°F. Trim the lamb of most of its fat and poke shallow holes with the tip of a sharp knife all over the surface. Place on a rack set within a roasting pan.

In a food processor or blender, combine ⅓ cup of the olive oil, the garlic, lemon juice, rosemary, and lavender. Pulse until the mixture is blended into a paste. Rub the lamb all over with the mixture, then season generously with salt and pepper.

Roast for 15 minutes. Decrease the oven temperature to 375°F. Toss the sweet potatoes and parsnips in the remaining olive oil and season with salt and pepper. Scatter in the bottom of the roasting pan and continue baking for 70 minutes longer, or until a thermometer inserted into the thickest part of the leg reads 135°F for medium-rare.

Transfer the lamb to a cutting board, cover, and let rest for 15 minutes before slicing against the grain. Arrange the meat on a platter and serve with the vegetables and jam on the side.

make it ahead Make the sauce 5 days in advance and store it in an airtight container in the refrigerator. Trim and prepare the lamb with the rub up to 2 days in advance and place it in the roasting pan. Wrap it tightly and store it in the refrigerator. Bring the lamb to room temperature prior to roasting. Cut up the vegetables and store them in a bowl of water, tightly covered, in the refrigerator for up to 3 days.

tidbits A bone-in leg provides rich flavor and ends up being cost-effective, but can be intimidating because it is so large and seems difficult to carve. For a boneless leg of lamb, purchase a 5-pound boneless leg roast that is rolled and tied with kitchen twine. Prepare it the same way as the bone-in leg, but roast it for only 50 to 60 minutes after decreasing the temperature.

blood orange and honey-glazed ham

I associate glazed ham with Easter after years of my family ordering honey hams wrapped in gold tinfoil that we picked up from the local store. If your family usually enjoys ham on Thanksgiving or Christmas, this recipe will work wonderfully for those holidays, as well. My favorite part about a large glazed ham is using it for leftovers, so this recipe intentionally yields more than 8 servings.

SERVES 12

1 (8- to 10-pound) bone-in, skin-on smoked uncured ham

Fine sea salt and freshly ground black pepper

½ cup ghee (page 325), grass-fed unsalted butter, or coconut oil

Finely grated zest and juice of 3 blood oranges

½ cup light-colored raw honey

¼ cup whole-grain mustard

8 fresh sage leaves

¼ teaspoon ground cloves

¼ teaspoon ground cinnamon

2 pounds baby carrots, cleaned and trimmed

1 blood orange, sliced, for garnish (optional)

Preheat the oven to 300°F.

Using a sharp knife, score the skin and fat of the ham in a 2-inch diamond pattern. Place the ham, fat side up, on a roasting rack in a roasting pan. Season generously with salt and pepper. Bake the ham for 1½ hours.

Meanwhile, make the glaze. Combine the ghee, orange juice, orange zest, honey, mustard, sage, cloves, and cinnamon in a small saucepan. Simmer for 30 minutes, or until the mixture has thickened into a syrup.

Increase the oven temperature to 350°F and remove the roasting pan. Season the carrots with salt and pepper and scatter them around the bottom of the roasting pan. Baste the ham with the glaze and return the pan to the oven. Bake for another 30 minutes, basting occasionally, until a meat thermometer inserted into the center of the ham reads 135°F and the carrots are tender.

Transfer the ham to a cutting board, cover, and let it rest for 20 minutes before carving. Serve the carrots on the side and place slices of blood orange decoratively around the platter for garnish.

make it ahead Make the glaze 3 days in advance and store it in an airtight container in the refrigerator. Reheat the glaze in a saucepan over low heat. Season the ham and place it in the roasting pan, covered with plastic wrap, in the refrigerator the night before. Clean and trim the carrots up to 2 days in advance and store them in a bowl of water, tightly covered, in the refrigerator. Alternatively, bake and slice the ham the morning of the brunch and spoon the juices onto the bottom of a platter. Arrange the ham and carrots on top, then cover and leave at room temperature for up to 2 hours. Reheat in a low oven just prior to serving.

tidbits Leftovers usually abound with large baked hams, so use the excess in Eggs Benedict Strata (page 113), atop pizza with pineapple (see page 72), or between two slices of blender bread (page 323).

sweet potato orange cups

My great-grandmother served these sweet potato cups every Easter, and my grandmother has carried on the tradition. Warming the sweet potato puree inside the orange cups imparts a divine orange flavor and also makes a cute presentation. These cups can be prepped in advance (see Make It Ahead), which is so helpful when you are preparing a meal with a large menu.

SERVES 8

4 large navel oranges

2½ pounds sweet potatoes, halved crosswise

¼ cup ghee (page 325) or coconut oil

½ cup freshly squeezed orange juice

¼ cup coconut sugar

¼ cup full-fat coconut milk

½ teaspoon fine sea salt

¼ cup chopped pecans

Preheat the oven to 350°F.

Slice a thin piece of the peel off each end of the oranges to make flat surfaces so the halves will stand upright. Cut the oranges in half, then working over a bowl to catch the juices, scoop out the pulp with a reamer or spoon, leaving only the shell. Squeeze the orange membranes into the bowl to extract any additional juices and discard the pulp.

Put the sweet potatoes in a pot of cold water. Bring the water to a boil over high heat and cook for 10 to 15 minutes, until the sweet potatoes are fork-tender. Drain and let cool slightly. Peel the potatoes and discard any fibrous strings. Put them in the bowl of a stand mixer fitted with the beater attachment, or use an electric handheld mixer. Beat to mash slightly, then add the ghee, orange juice, coconut sugar, coconut milk, and salt. Beat the sweet potatoes until smooth and creamy.

Fill each orange cup with the sweet potato mixture and top with the pecans. Place them on a large rimmed baking sheet and bake, uncovered, for 20 minutes, or until heated through. Serve hot.

make it ahead The orange cups can be prepared and filled up to 3 days in advance. Cover and refrigerate, then bake as directed before serving.

carrot cake

What is an Easter brunch, or any spring celebration for that matter, without a classic carrot cake? I adore the trio of cinnamon, ginger, and nutmeg in this cake and also love the shredded coconut and raisins. If you use the cream cheese frosting, this cake is also tree nut-free.

SERVES 8

½ cup palm shortening

¼ cup full-fat coconut milk

¾ cup cooked and mashed sweet potato

½ cup arrowroot powder

5 tablespoons coconut flour

1½ teaspoons grain-free baking powder (page 325)

½ teaspoon baking soda

1 teaspoon ground cinnamon

1 teaspoon ground ginger

¾ teaspoon ground nutmeg

½ teaspoon fine sea salt

½ cup pure maple syrup

2 teaspoons pure vanilla extract

3 eggs, at room temperature

1¼ cups peeled and shredded carrots (about 2 medium carrots)

¼ cup unsweetened shredded dried coconut

¼ cup raisins

2 teaspoons freshly squeezed lemon juice

½ cup whipped cream (page 332) or Cream Cheese Frosting (page 163)

Preheat the oven to 325°F. Lightly grease two 6 by 3-inch round cake pans with palm shortening and place a round piece of parchment paper at the bottom of each pan.

Melt the shortening in the coconut milk in a small saucepan over medium heat.

In a stand mixer fitted with the beater attachment, or using an electric handheld mixer, combine the sweet potato, arrowroot powder, coconut flour, baking powder, baking soda, cinnamon, ginger, nutmeg, and salt and beat for 30 seconds. Pour the hot coconut milk mixture into the bowl and add the maple syrup and vanilla. Beat on high for 30 seconds, or until smooth. Add the eggs, one at a time, beating well after each addition. Stir in the carrots, shredded coconut, raisins, and lemon juice. Divide the batter between the two prepared pans. Bake for 35 minutes, or until a toothpick inserted into the center of the cake comes out clean.

Cool on a wire rack for 20 minutes. Loosen the sides with a knife, then invert the pans to remove the cakes. Cool the cakes completely, right side up. Place one cake round on a plate or pedestal and spread the whipped cream on top. Place the other cake round on top. Store the cake in the refrigerator until you are ready to serve.

make it ahead The unfrosted cakes can be stored in the refrigerator for up to 3 days, or in the freezer for up to 6 months. Bring to room temperature before layering and frosting.

tidbits The batter can be baked in a 9-inch round cake pan or a 12-cavity muffin pan lined with paper cupcake liners for 20 to 25 minutes.

Use an orange-fleshed sweet potato, or yam, to get the beautiful orange hue.

For a fully frosted cake, use an additional ½ cup whipped cream or cream cheese frosting to frost the sides and top of the cake. Top with 2 tablespoons unsweetened dried, flaked coconut.

lavender lemonade

A mild, light honey sweetens this lavender-infused lemonade, creating a refreshing drink for your springtime gatherings. Culinary lavender can be found at most health food stores or ordered online in bulk.

SERVES 8

6 cups water

½ cup light-colored raw honey

⅓ cup dried lavender

1 cup freshly squeezed lemon juice, strained

Ice, for serving

8 lemon slices, for garnish

Warm the water and honey in a pot over medium-high heat until the honey dissolves into the water. Gently crush the lavender in a mortar and pestle or in a bowl with a meat tenderizer. Add the crushed lavender to the pot, then remove the pot from the heat.

Cover, refrigerate, and let steep for 2 hours.

Strain the liquid through a fine-mesh sieve into a pitcher. Stir in the lemon juice and serve over ice with a lemon slice in each glass.

make it ahead Store the lemonade in a covered pitcher in the refrigerator for up to 1 week.

mother's day
luncheon

Since Ryan and I have been together, we have had a Mother's Day tradition of going to brunch with Ryan's family at a scenic restaurant high atop the hills in Napa Valley. The four-course meal is always as stunning as the scenery. However, when I celebrate Mother's Day with my family, I tend to be the one to prepare most of the food. I enjoy hosting brunch for my mom and grandmother, as well as for my sisters, who have recently become mothers, too.

The moms in my family like to have a little bit of breakfast served alongside a light lunch and then finish with a springtime treat. My mom and I both love eggs Benedict but do not love the time it takes to individually prepare them for a party. To relieve the stress, I make a Benedict casserole drizzled with the quintessential velvety hollandaise sauce. A light salad of spring berries and salmon and warm asparagus soup with a poached egg on top make the meal feel special and complete. And since both my mom and mother-in-law are lemon-lovers, I finish the meal with tart lemon bars.

Because our Mother's Day celebrations are more intimate affairs, I've created the recipes in this chapter to feed eight. Although I love celebrating the other mothers in my life, I look forward to the day when my boys have learned enough from me to cook a Mother's Day brunch of their own.

Happy Mother's Day!

menu

❖❖❖

Asparagus and Leek Soup
with a Poached Egg

Eggs Benedict Strata

Strawberry Salmon Salad
with Poppy Seed Dressing

❖❖❖

Lemon Bars

❖❖❖

Ginger Peach Sangria

asparagus and leek soup with a poached egg

There's no dairy cream in this soup, but it is so smooth you would never know it. A poached egg on soup may seem a bit odd, but the richness of the runny yolk with the creamy soup is absolutely wonderful and satisfying.

SERVES 8

3 tablespoons ghee (page 325) or coconut oil

2 cups chopped leeks, white and tender green parts

2 cloves garlic, minced

2 pounds asparagus, trimmed and cut into 1-inch pieces

½ cup peeled and cubed Hannah sweet potato or other white-fleshed variety

4 cups chicken stock (page 327)

1½ teaspoons fine sea salt

¼ teaspoon freshly ground black pepper, plus more to sprinkle

2 teaspoons apple cider vinegar

8 eggs

tidbits To poach the eggs in the oven, preheat it to 350°F. Pour 1 tablespoon water and ¼ teaspoon vinegar into each of 8 cavities of a muffin pan. Crack an egg into each cavity and poach in the oven for 8 to 10 minutes, until the whites are cooked through and the yolks are still soft. Gently scoop the eggs out and drain on a paper towel-lined plate.

Heat the ghee in a large stockpot over medium heat. Add the leeks and sauté for 3 to 4 minutes, stirring constantly, until the leeks are fragrant and softened. Add the garlic, asparagus, and sweet potato and continue cooking for 5 minutes. Pour in the stock and bring to a boil. Reduce the heat and simmer for 10 to 12 minutes, until the potatoes and asparagus are fork-tender.

Working in batches, ladle the soup into a blender (see Tidbits, page 26) and blend on high for 60 seconds, or until smooth. Return the soup to the pan, season with the salt and pepper, and keep warm.

To poach the eggs, add 3 inches of water to a deep saucepan and bring to a boil. Add the vinegar to the water and lower the heat so the water is simmering gently. Crack each egg into its own little bowl. Working in batches of 3 or 4 eggs at a time, carefully slide each egg into the water. Cover the pan and remove from the heat. Poach the eggs for 7 to 8 minutes, until the whites are fully cooked. Remove the eggs with a slotted spoon and place on a plate lined with a paper towel. Bring the water back up to simmering and repeat with the remaining eggs.

Serve each bowl of soup with a poached egg on top and a sprinkle of fresh pepper.

make it ahead Make the soup up to 3 days in advance and reheat over medium-low heat. To freeze, refrigerate the soup until cool, then freeze in an airtight container for up to 3 months. Thaw the soup in the refrigerator overnight, then reheat as above.

Poach the eggs up to 3 days in advance and store immersed in water in an airtight container in the refrigerator. Reheat in a pot of water over medium-low heat for 5 minutes.

eggs benedict strata

Eggs Benedict is a special dish, and I love to serve it for holidays. However, standing over the stove to poach a dozen eggs is time-consuming and can be daunting for most cooks, so I came up with this easy overnight casserole to feed a crowd. With a fresh hollandaise sauce drizzled over the top, this dish feels every bit as singular but requires half the work.

SERVES 8

2 cups blender bread (page 323), in ½-inch cubes

12 ounces ham, cut into ¼-inch cubes

8 eggs

¾ cup full-fat coconut milk

½ cup almond milk (page 320)

1¼ teaspoons fine sea salt

¾ teaspoon onion powder

½ teaspoon sweet paprika

2 tablespoons chopped fresh chives

hollandaise sauce

4 egg yolks

½ cup palm shortening or ghee (page 325), melted

1 tablespoon freshly squeezed lemon juice

½ teaspoon fine sea salt

½ teaspoon sweet paprika

Combine the bread cubes and ham in the bottom of a lightly greased 9 by 13-inch baking dish. In a bowl, whisk together the eggs, coconut milk, almond milk, salt, onion powder, and paprika. Pour the mixture over the bread and ham, cover, and place in the refrigerator overnight.

Pull the baking dish out of the refrigerator and leave at room temperature while the oven preheats to 375°F. Gently stir the bread and ham to ensure it is fully coated in the egg mixture, then bake, uncovered, for 30 minutes.

Meanwhile, make the hollandaise sauce. Fill a saucepan halfway with water and heat over medium-high heat. Place a heatproof bowl over the saucepan to create a double-boiler setup; make sure that the bottom of the bowl does not touch the water. Whisk the egg yolks vigorously in the bowl over the heat until pale in color and thickened slightly, about 2 minutes.

Slowly drizzle in the melted palm shortening, whisking continuously. Continue whisking until the sauce has thickened and doubled in volume. Remove from the heat and whisk in the lemon juice, salt, and paprika.

When the strata is ready, remove from the oven and cut into 8 pieces. Serve hot with the warm hollandaise drizzled over the top.

make it ahead The hollandaise sauce can be made up to 2 days in advance and stored in an airtight container in the refrigerator. Reheat it slowly over a double boiler on low heat.

tidbits Swap the ham for lump crabmeat for a delicious crab Benedict strata or add baby spinach to make a Florentine strata.

If the hollandaise breaks, whisk in 1 tablespoon of cold water at a time until it comes together.

strawberry salmon salad with poppy seed dressing

This salad is refreshing and colorful, with wild salmon fillets topping a bowl of bright leafy spinach and tart strawberries. I think every salad needs a crunchy component, so thinly sliced almonds and red onions are added just before it is tossed with the poppy seed dressing.

SERVES 8

8 (4-ounce) skinless wild salmon fillets

Coarse sea salt and freshly ground black pepper

1¼ pounds baby spinach

1 pint strawberries, hulled and quartered

½ small red onion, thinly sliced

¼ cup sliced almonds

dressing

¼ cup light-colored raw honey

¼ cup champagne vinegar

1 tablespoon grated shallot

1 tablespoon poppy seeds

2 teaspoons Dijon mustard

1 teaspoon freshly squeezed lemon juice

½ cup macadamia nut oil

¼ cup extra-virgin olive oil

Salt and freshly ground black pepper

Preheat the broiler with the rack in the upper third of the oven, about 4 inches from the broiler. Line a rimmed baking sheet with parchment paper.

Place the salmon fillets on the prepared baking sheet and season them with the salt and pepper. Broil for 10 to 12 minutes, until the salmon flakes easily. Set aside to cool.

To make the dressing, whisk together the honey, vinegar, shallot, poppy seeds, mustard, and lemon juice. While whisking constantly, slowly drizzle in the macadamia oil, then the olive oil. Continue whisking until well incorporated. Season with salt and pepper.

In a large bowl, toss the spinach with the strawberries, onion, almonds, and ½ cup of the dressing. Divide the salad among plates and place a salmon fillet atop each. Serve the additional dressing on the side.

make it ahead Make the dressing up to 1 week in advance and store in an airtight container in the refrigerator. Bring the dressing to room temperature and shake it vigorously before using.

lemon bars

Lemon bars are the perfect ending to a spring brunch, and they're even easy enough for kids to make as a special Mother's Day treat. These bars have a nut-free shortbread crust and a tart lemon filling. In place of the powdered sugar that is usually sprinkled on top to balance the sour lemon, I top mine with finely shredded unsweetened coconut or fresh berries for a bit of sweetness.

MAKES 12 BARS

crust

¾ cup coconut flour

½ cup arrowroot powder

½ cup palm shortening, ghee (page 325), or coconut oil

¼ cup maple sugar

½ teaspoon pure vanilla extract

½ teaspoon fine sea salt

2 eggs

filling

9 eggs, lightly beaten

1 cup plus 2 tablespoons freshly squeezed lemon juice

¾ cup light-colored raw honey

6 tablespoons arrowroot powder

1 tablespoon finely grated lemon zest

½ teaspoon fine sea salt

¼ cup finely shredded unsweetened dried coconut, or 1 cup sliced fresh strawberries or raspberries, for topping

Preheat the oven to 350°F. Lightly grease a 9 by 13-inch baking dish with coconut oil.

To make the crust, in a stand mixer fitted with the beater attachment, or using an electric handheld mixer, combine the coconut flour, arrowroot, palm shortening, maple sugar, vanilla extract, and salt and beat on medium speed until mixed. Add the eggs and beat on medium-high speed until the eggs are fully incorporated and a loose dough forms. Press the dough into the bottom of the prepared baking dish, making sure to press it slightly up the sides of the dish so the lemon filling doesn't seep beneath. Bake for 15 minutes.

To make the filling, in a bowl, whisk together the eggs, lemon juice, honey, arrowroot, lemon zest, and salt until evenly blended. Pour the filling onto the hot crust and return the pan to the oven. Bake for 15 minutes longer, or until the center is almost set but still jiggles slightly. Turn off the heat and cool in the oven with the door cracked open for 20 minutes.

Chill completely in the refrigerator before serving. Slice into bars or squares and serve topped with the coconut.

make it ahead Make these bars 3 days in advance and store them, tightly wrapped, in the refrigerator. Sprinkle the coconut or place the berries on top just prior to serving.

tidbits The bars may not look completely done when you turn off the oven, but stopping the baking a tiny bit early will help prevent the tops from cracking.

ginger peach sangria

When I think of a spring beverage to serve for a brunch or a luncheon, I want something that is fresh and fruity, and a little sweet. This effervescent sangria uses sweet stone fruits and ginger ale to create a lovely refreshing beverage for moms to enjoy on their special day. Sparkling water can be substituted for the ginger ale for a mildly sweet cocktail.

SERVES 6

1 (750-ml) bottle dry white wine, such as Sauvignon Blanc or Pinot Grigio

½ cup 100-proof apple brandy

½ cup peach puree (see Tidbits)

2 tablespoons light-colored raw honey, melted

2 peaches, pitted and sliced

2 plums, pitted and sliced

1½ cups Ginger Ale (page 181) or any store-bought natural, unfiltered ginger ale

10 small fresh basil leaves or mint leaves, plus more for garnish

Ice, for serving

In a large pitcher or punch bowl, combine the wine, brandy, peach puree, and honey. Stir in the peach and plum slices. Cover and place in the refrigerator overnight to chill and allow the flavors to meld.

Remove the pitcher from the refrigerator and stir in the ginger ale and basil leaves just prior to serving. Pour into 6 glasses filled with ice and garnish with a small basil leaf.

tidbits To make the peach puree, defrost 5 ounces frozen peaches and place them in a blender. Blend on medium-high speed until smooth. Alternatively, peel and remove the pits from 2 medium peaches. Cut them into chunks and blend in a blender on medium-high speed until smooth.

father's day
cookout

menu

◆◆◆

*Knife-and-Fork
Pork Ribs*

*Tri-Tip with
Grilled Vegetables
and Chimichurri Sauce*

Baked "Beans"

Skillet "Corn" Bread

◆◆◆

Peach Cobbler

◆◆◆

Margarita

All three of the dads in my life—my dad, my father-in-law, and my husband, Ryan—are big barbecue lovers. Because good barbecue restaurants are not as prevalent in California as they are in Austin or Kansas City, I make a point of firing up the grill at home to honor my favorite guys on their special day with a big backyard cookout.

My grandmother taught me that it's always a good idea to have more than one protein option at a barbecue in case one person doesn't eat pork or another takes too much of the sliced meat (hello, Ryan). Plus, with all of the tantalizing smells coming from the grill, it's hard to choose just one type of meat. When I eat barbecue out, I always end up ordering the combo plate so I can try a bit of each.

Served with classic side dishes like "beans" and "corn" bread, washed down with a refreshing margarita, and finished with a summery peach cobbler, this meal of fall-off-the-bone ribs and marinated tri-tip is sure to please every dad in your life.

Happy Father's Day!

knife-and-fork pork ribs

My husband, Ryan's, favorite dinner is a rack of fork-tender ribs from a local restaurant where we have been celebrating his birthdays since high school. So I make him homemade ribs each year for Father's Day. Barbecued ribs are typically cooked slowly in a smoker, but these ribs are tender and flavorful from slow cooking in the oven, and they can be finished either on the grill for a smoky crust or put under the broiler for ease. I've included our favorite barbecue sauce, or check out the Tidbits below for a super simple and quick sauce.

SERVES 8

½ cup coconut sugar

2 tablespoons sweet paprika

2 tablespoons chili powder

2 tablespoons garlic powder

1 tablespoon fine sea salt

1 teaspoon freshly ground black pepper

2 (4-pound) pork baby back rib racks

2 cups barbecue sauce (page 321)

Preheat the oven to 250°F.

Mix together the coconut sugar, paprika, chili powder, garlic powder, salt, and pepper to make a dry rub. Rub 2 tablespoons of the rub on each rack, then place each rack on a large sheet of parchment paper. (Reserve the remaining rub in an airtight container at room temperature for another use.) Wrap the ribs tightly and roll up the ends of the paper to create a tightly sealed parchment paper package. Place the packages with the meat facing down on two rimmed baking sheets. Bake for 3 to 3½ hours, or until fork-tender.

Preheat a grill to medium-high heat or preheat the broiler with the rack placed in the upper one-third of the oven.

Open the parchment packages and drain off any fat and liquid. Turn the ribs so the meat is facing up, brush them with some of the barbecue sauce, and finish on the grill over direct heat for 5 minutes, or under the broiler for 2 to 3 minutes, until browned and slightly crisp on top. Serve warm with the remaining barbecue sauce on the side.

make it ahead Season the ribs 3 days in advance and store them, tightly wrapped, in the refrigerator. Bake the racks 2 days in advance and keep them covered. Reheat in a 300°F oven for 15 minutes, then finish under the broiler or on the grill.

tidbits For a quick barbecue sauce, whisk together 2 cups tomato puree, ½ cup of the leftover dry rub, 6 tablespoons white wine vinegar, 6 tablespoons coconut sugar, 2 tablespoons tomato paste, 2 teaspoons Dijon mustard, and ¾ teaspoon natural liquid smoke.

beef

2 whole tri-tip roasts, about 2 pounds each

½ cup extra-virgin olive oil

¼ cup coconut aminos

1 small shallot, minced

2 cloves garlic, minced

1 tablespoon coconut sugar

2 teaspoons freshly squeezed lime juice

1 teaspoon fine sea salt

½ teaspoon dried red pepper flakes

½ teaspoon ground cumin

vegetables

4 zucchini, thinly sliced lengthwise

4 patty pan squashes, halved lengthwise

2 red bell peppers, seeded and thinly sliced

2 Japanese eggplants, thinly sliced lengthwise

1 bunch asparagus, ends trimmed

1 small yellow onion, thinly sliced

¼ cup extra-virgin olive oil

1 tablespoon freshly squeezed lemon juice

½ teaspoon fine sea salt

½ teaspoon freshly ground black pepper

Chimichurri sauce (page 324), for serving

tri-tip with grilled vegetables and chimichurri sauce

I love to prepare a beef roast on the grill when I'm hosting a large party because it is easier to manage than multiple steaks. This tri-tip sits in a flavorful marinade before grilling and is served with a medley of grilled vegetables and a bright Argentine herb sauce.

To prepare the beef, place the roasts in a nonreactive dish and poke a few shallow holes all over the meat with a sharp knife. Whisk together the olive oil, coconut aminos, shallot, garlic, coconut sugar, lime juice, salt, red pepper flakes, and cumin in a small bowl and pour over the roasts. Cover tightly and refrigerate for at least 6 hours or up to 24 hours. Turn the meat occasionally in the marinade.

Preheat a grill to medium heat. Remove the roasts from the marinade and shake off any excess liquid. Place them over the hottest area of the grill, cover, and cook for 5 minutes. Turn the roasts and continue grilling for 5 minutes. Move the roasts to a cooler area of the grill and continue cooking with the lid on for 15 to 20 minutes more, or until a thermometer reads 130°F for medium-rare when inserted into the thickest part of the roasts. Cover loosely and set aside to rest.

To prepare the vegetables, toss the zucchini, patty pan squash, red bell peppers, eggplants, asparagus, and onion with the olive oil, lemon juice, salt, and pepper. Grill the vegetables in a metal roasting pan or vegetable grill basket, flipping once halfway through, for about 4 minutes per side, or until tender and lightly charred.

Transfer the meat and vegetables to a cutting board and thinly slice the meat against the grain. Serve the meat and vegetables hot with the chimichurri sauce spooned over the top.

make it ahead Prepare and toss the vegetables up to 2 days in advance and store them in an airtight container in the refrigerator.

tidbits Carve the meat against the grain for a tender tri-tip. Inspect the meat before marinating and grilling, and once it's cooked, slice the roasts in half where the grain changes direction and carve each piece separately.

If you can't find or special order a tri-tip, substitute flank steak or skirt steak.

baked "beans"

Legumes are avoided on a Paleo Diet, so I wanted to replace them with something that had a similar texture and consistency. Pine nuts may seem like a strange ingredient to find in a barbecue-flavored dish, but when cooked, they closely resemble beans. I remember seeing a contestant use pine nuts on one of my favorite cooking shows, *Top Chef*, and I was inspired to make my own recipe. I've used nuts as a replacement for many things over the years but hadn't thought to try them instead of beans!

SERVES 8

3 cups raw pine nuts (about 1 pound)

8 ounces thick-cut bacon

1 green bell pepper, seeded and diced

1 red bell pepper, seeded and diced

½ small yellow onion, diced

1 clove garlic, minced

¾ cup water

½ cup pure maple syrup

⅓ cup tomato paste

⅓ cup coconut sugar

3 tablespoons white vinegar

1½ teaspoons fine sea salt

¾ teaspoon powdered mustard

¾ teaspoon chili powder

¾ teaspoon sweet paprika

½ teaspoon ground allspice

Preheat the oven to 350°F.

Put the pine nuts in a large pot and cover with water. Bring to a boil and cook for 15 minutes. Drain and set aside.

Reserve 3 slices of bacon and dice the remaining pieces. Cook the diced bacon in a large Dutch oven set over medium-high heat until crisp, about 5 minutes. Add the bell peppers, onion, and garlic and sauté for 5 to 7 minutes, until the vegetables are crisp-tender. Stir in the cooked pine nuts and the water, maple syrup, tomato paste, coconut sugar, white vinegar, salt, powdered mustard, chili powder, paprika, and allspice. Turn the mixture out into a 9 by 13-inch baking dish and top with the reserved strips of bacon.

Cover and bake for 30 minutes, then uncover and bake for an additional 45 minutes, or until the bacon is crisp and the pine nuts are tender. Allow the dish to cool for 15 minutes, then serve warm.

make it ahead Store the unbaked dish in the refrigerator for up to 3 days or in the freezer for up to 6 months. Bring to room temperature before baking as directed.

tidbits Costco often carries organic pine nuts, or find good prices through online retailers and Trader Joe's.

skillet "corn" bread

Warm cornbread with butter and raw, creamy honey was always one of my favorite treats to eat during summer barbecues, or during the colder months with a bowl of chili. After realizing that corn caused me extreme bloating and discomfort, I came up with this recipe to replace the old version I used to love.

SERVES 8 TO 10

¼ cup palm shortening or ghee (page 325)

¾ cup almond milk (page 320)

¼ cup light-colored raw honey

1 teaspoon apple cider vinegar

5 eggs

2¼ cups blanched almond flour

¼ cup coconut flour

1 teaspoon grain-free baking powder (page 325)

½ teaspoon baking soda

½ teaspoon fine sea salt

Preheat the oven to 350°F. Heat the palm shortening in a 10-inch cast-iron skillet over medium-high heat until melted. Swirl it around to coat the bottom and sides of the skillet, then pour the melted shortening into the bowl of a stand mixer fitted with the beater attachment, or use an electric handheld mixer. Place the cast-iron skillet back on the stove top and keep on low heat.

Add the almond milk, honey, and vinegar to the mixing bowl and mix on medium speed for 30 seconds. Add the eggs, one at a time, beating well after each addition. Add the almond flour, coconut flour, baking powder, baking soda, and salt and mix until combined. Pour the batter into the hot cast-iron skillet.

Bake for 30 minutes, or until the bread is golden and a toothpick inserted into the center of the bread comes out clean. Cool for 30 minutes on a wire rack and serve warm.

make it ahead Once the bread has cooled completely, tightly wrap it in the pan and store it in the refrigerator for up to 1 week. Serve it chilled, or reheat it in the pan in a 300°F oven for 15 minutes.

peach cobbler

When I polled all of my readers about which summer dessert they would want to see most in this book, it came as no surprise that a peach cobbler was the overwhelming choice. Cobblers of any sort just scream summer to me, so creating a cobbler recipe has long been on my short list. I love the subtle flavor of the cashew in this warm biscuit topping, and the taste of cooked peaches is just divine.

SERVES 8

6 tablespoons ghee (page 325) or coconut oil

8 yellow peaches, pitted and sliced (about 2 pounds)

¼ cup light-colored raw honey

1 tablespoon freshly squeezed lemon juice

¼ teaspoon ground cinnamon

¼ teaspoon ground nutmeg

1 cup raw cashew butter

¼ cup arrowroot powder

¼ cup plus 1 tablespoon coconut flour

¾ cup maple sugar

1 tablespoon grain-free baking powder (page 325)

¾ cup full-fat coconut milk

Whipped cream (page 332) or whipped coconut cream (page 331), for serving

Preheat the oven to 350°F. Put the ghee in a 9 by 13-inch baking dish and place it in the oven to melt.

Combine the sliced peaches, honey, lemon juice, cinnamon, and nutmeg in a saucepan and bring to a boil. Reduce the heat to low and simmer for 10 minutes.

Combine the cashew butter, arrowroot, coconut flour, maple sugar, baking powder, and coconut milk in a stand mixer fitted with the beater attachment or use an electric handheld mixer. Mix on medium speed until well combined.

To assemble, spoon the peach mixture into the hot baking dish. Spoon dollops of batter over the top.

Bake for 40 minutes, or until the top is golden brown. Serve warm with whipped cream.

make it ahead The cobbler can be assembled up to 2 days in advance and stored, tightly wrapped, in the refrigerator. Bring to room temperature before baking.

tidbits I never peel my peaches for cobbler because I love the color and tart flavor that the skin imparts, but you're welcome to peel them before cooking, if you prefer.

Frozen sliced peaches can be substituted for the fresh peaches. There is no need to thaw them before putting them in the saucepan.

margarita

My brother, Joel, is an awesome cocktail maker with an impressive home bar, and he created this refined sugar-free version of the classic cocktail. My maiden name is Norsworthy, so we call these WorthyBar Margs, and they have been enjoyed at family celebrations for years. He also shared this recipe on my blog a few years back, and it has been a huge fan favorite ever since.

SERVES 1

Flaked sea salt, for garnish

Lime wedge, for moistening rim and garnish

½ cup ice cubes, plus more for serving

2 ounces blanco tequila (100 percent agave)

1 ounce freshly squeezed lime juice

1 ounce honey syrup (see Tidbits, page 43)

For a salted rim, pour a thin layer of salt flakes onto a plate or cutting board. Use the lime wedge to lightly moisten the rim of a glass before flipping it over into the salt to coat. Fill the glass three-fourths full with ice.

Combine the tequila, lime juice, and honey syrup in a cocktail shaker and add the ½ cup ice. Shake vigorously for 10 seconds. Pour through a fine-mesh sieve into the prepared glass. Add the lime wedge and serve.

make it ahead To make a pitcher of margaritas, combine 2 cups tequila, 1 cup lime juice, 1 cup honey syrup, and ½ cup cold water in a pitcher. Stir to combine. Refrigerate for up to 2 days, then stir in 2 cups ice cubes before pouring.

tidbits Tequila makes a great grain-free and gluten-free cocktail. Be sure to use 100 percent agave tequila, which means there is no added sugar or water.

birthday party

menu

◆◆◆

Burger Bites

Mini "Corn" Dog Muffins

AB&J Hand Sandwiches

Fruit Kabobs

Veggie Cups

◆◆◆

Chocolate Cake

Red Velvet Cake

Nut-Free Yellow Cake

Yellow Cake

Strawberry Cake

Vanilla Cake

◆◆◆

Vanilla Buttercream

Chocolate Buttercream

Raspberry Buttercream

Diary-Free Cream Cheese Frosting

Cream Cheese Frosting

Quick Chocolate Icing

A child's birthday party, or any birthday party for that matter, can be a big source of anxiety when celebrating with or for people who have food restrictions. You don't want your child or other grain-free guests to feel ostracized by serving them something different from the other guests, but you also don't want to make a menu that not everyone will enjoy.

This collection of fun finger foods has passed both the child and the parent test. My son Asher and his friends love all of these dishes, and even their parents give these a thumbs up. I like to serve a buffet of small bites at a child's birthday party so the kids can grab a few things and go play, then come back for more when they get hungry. Your littles will love my take on corn dogs and burgers, and what is a child's party without PB&J sandwiches (or AB&J, in our case)? I particularly love the fruit skewers dipped in my newest favorite condiment, my whipped cream (page 332). With other parents, grandparents, and aunts and uncles attending as well, I always make a point of creating food that is both child-friendly and filling enough for adults.

Since the birthday cake is the most important part of the party for most kids (and some adults), I spent a lot of time experimenting to give you the perfect birthday cake recipe. Let's face it, transforming your family's favorite cake recipe is not as easy as a simple substitution. Since all children have a favorite flavor, I've provided the classics here (chocolate, vanilla, yellow, strawberry, and red velvet cakes paired with frostings), along with a few nut-free options. Mix and match to create the perfect combination for your event. You can even turn these cake recipes into cupcakes.

For adults who want a more refined menu for their parties, choose dishes from any of the chapters in this book to create the perfect birthday party spread. If you have a barbecue-loving guy, you may opt for the Father's Day meal on page 123 or the Fourth of July menu on page 167. For a lady's birthday luncheon, try combining some of the menu items from the Easter brunch (page 87) and the summer shower (page 185).

I wish each of you a happy birthday!

burger bites

When my oldest son, Asher, was younger, he would eat pretty much anything on a toothpick, so we skewered all sorts of meals. He still prefers to eat a burger without even a grain-free bun, so these little burger bites have been a favorite of his for many years.

MAKES 30 BITES

2 pounds grass-fed ground beef

8 ounces bacon, minced

2 tablespoons prepared yellow mustard

½ teaspoon fine sea salt

½ teaspoon onion powder

¼ teaspoon freshly ground black pepper

1 head butter lettuce

30 cherry tomatoes

30 dill pickle chips

Ketchup (page 328), mayonnaise (page 328), and mustard, for serving

Preheat a grill to medium-high heat.

Using your hands or a stand mixer fitted with the beater attachment, gently knead together the beef, bacon, mustard, salt, onion powder, and pepper. Form the mixture into 30 golf ball–size meatballs.

Place the meatballs on the grill, searing them on all sides to brown. Reduce the heat to medium-low or move the meatballs to indirect heat away from the coals and grill, covered, for 4 to 6 minutes, until a meat thermometer inserted into the center of a meatball reads 145°F for medium doneness.

To create the burger bites, remove the core from the lettuce and cut the leaves into bite-size pieces. Thread the lettuce, tomatoes, pickles, and meatballs onto 4-inch bamboo skewers. Cut off the pointed tips after threading for safety. Serve with the condiments on the side for dipping.

make it ahead Prepare the meatballs up to 3 days in advance and store them, tightly covered, in the refrigerator. Bring to room temperature before grilling. Skewer the lettuce, tomato, and pickles the night before the party and place them on a platter with a barely damp paper towel covering them. Tightly wrap the platter and store in the refrigerator. Add the grilled burgers just before you're ready to serve.

tidbits Grass-fed beef tends to be on the lean side. Gently kneading the beef mixture keeps the meatballs juicy and flavorful.

mini "corn" dog muffins

These bite-size, sweet, and crispy muffins with savory, grass-fed beef hot dogs are hard to resist, especially when dunked in ketchup.

3 eggs

⅓ cup almond milk (page 320)

2 tablespoons light-colored raw honey

2 tablespoons melted ghee (page 325) or coconut oil

½ teaspoon apple cider vinegar

1¼ cups blanched almond flour

½ teaspoon grain-free baking powder (page 325)

¼ teaspoon baking soda

¼ teaspoon fine sea salt

2 tablespoons coconut flour

6 grass-fed all-beef hot dogs, cut into 1-inch pieces

Ketchup (page 328), for serving

Preheat the oven to 350°F. Lightly grease a 24-cavity mini muffin pan.

Combine the eggs, almond milk, honey, ghee, vinegar, almond flour, baking powder, baking soda, and salt in a blender. Blend on medium speed for 30 seconds. Add the coconut flour and blend again for 30 seconds, or until smooth.

Scoop about 1 tablespoon of the batter into each muffin cavity and place a hot dog piece in the center of each. Bake for 25 minutes, until golden brown on top and cooked through. Cool on a wire rack for 20 minutes, then remove from the pan and serve warm with the ketchup.

make it ahead Bake these muffins up to 3 days in advance, cool, and then remove from the muffin pan and store in an airtight container in the refrigerator. Place on a baking sheet and reheat in a 350°F oven for 10 minutes. To freeze the muffins, let cool to room temperature and freeze in a single layer on a baking sheet. Once frozen, transfer to an airtight container or bag and store in the freezer for up to 3 months. Reheat the frozen muffins in a 400°F oven for 15 minutes.

tidbits Look for grass-fed all-beef hot dogs that are nitrate-free.

ab&j hand sandwiches

What child's party is complete without the quintessential peanut butter and jelly sandwich? We use almond butter as our nut butter of choice, but sunflower seed butter or pecan butter will work as well. Beware, the parents will grab for these just as eagerly as the kiddos.

MAKES 8 SANDWICHES

1 cup unsweetened almond butter

1 cup unsweetened jam

1 loaf blender bread (page 323), cut into 16 slices

Spread almond butter and jam onto half of the bread slices and sandwich them with the other slices. Cut out desired shapes with cookie cutters, or simply cut in half and serve.

make it ahead Bake the bread and store it wrapped first in parchment paper and then tightly in plastic wrap for up to 5 days.

tidbits Look for unsweetened jams from St. Dalfour or Bionaturae, which are free from added sugars, or use a jam recipe from my blog againstallgrain.com.

fruit kabobs

Kids love to eat things on skewers, plus skewers are great for parties because they keep little hands from touching all of the other food before choosing the one they want. And by eliminating utensils, you make it easier to clean up.

SERVES 8

32 pieces assorted fruit, such as peach or mango slices, strawberries, blueberries, grapes, pineapple wedges, kiwi slices, and tangerine segments

Whipped cream (page 332), chilled

Thread 4 pieces of fruit onto each of eight 4-inch bamboo skewers. Cut off the pointed tips after threading for safety with very young children. Serve with the whipped cream for dipping.

tidbit Feel free to use your child's favorite fruits and what is in season at the time of your party.

veggie cups

With all of the sweets served at birthday parties, it's hard to get little ones to willingly reach for vegetables. Cutting veggies into sticks and having individual dipping cups of ranch dressing makes this vegetable option fun and inviting. This dressing is dairy-free, and tastes even better than the store-bought version most kids adore.

SERVES 8

2 cups herb ranch dressing (page 326)

24 small radishes, cleaned and stems on

8 small carrots, peeled and cut in half lengthwise

2 Persian cucumbers, cut into 6-inch spears

Pour 2 tablespoons of the dressing into the bottom of 8 small cups. Stand up the radishes, carrots, and cucumbers in the cups so the ends are dipped in the dressing.

make it ahead The dressing can be stored in a jar in the refrigerator for up to 5 days. Prep and cut the vegetables up to 2 days in advance and store in a bowl of water, tightly covered, in the refrigerator to keep fresh.

tidbits If your child has a favorite vegetable, feel free to substitute his or her favorite here. Snap peas, jicama sticks, or cherry tomatoes threaded onto party toothpicks are all great choices.

From left: yellow cake,
red velvet cake, strawberry cake,
and chocolate cake

chocolate cake

Using Dutch-processed cocoa powder makes this nut-free cake rich and full of dark chocolate flavors (pictured on page 151). It is my favorite cake in the book because it is decadent and moist. I love to keep it simple and frost this cake with Vanilla Buttercream (page 160), but a double-chocolate cake with Quick Chocolate Icing (page 163) would be luxurious.

SERVES 8

½ cup palm shortening, softened

½ cup coconut sugar

¼ cup pure maple syrup

1 teaspoon pure vanilla extract

1 teaspoon freshly squeezed lemon juice

3 eggs

¼ cup arrowroot powder

½ cup Dutch-processed cocoa powder

½ cup coconut flour

¾ teaspoon baking soda

¼ teaspoon fine sea salt

¾ cup full-fat coconut milk

Preheat the oven to 325°F. Lightly grease two 6 by 3-inch cake pans with palm shortening and place a round piece of parchment paper at the bottom of each pan.

In the bowl of a stand mixer fitted with the beater attachment, or using an electric handheld mixer, cream together the palm shortening, coconut sugar, maple syrup, vanilla, and lemon juice on medium speed for 1 minute. Add the eggs, one at a time, mixing well after each addition.

Whisk together the arrowroot, cocoa powder, coconut flour, baking soda, and salt in a small bowl. Alternate adding the dry mixture and the coconut milk to the mixer bowl until fully incorporated, mixing after each addition on medium-high speed. Divide the batter between the prepared pans.

Bake for 30 to 35 minutes, until a toothpick inserted into the center of the cakes comes out clean.

Cool the cakes on a wire rack for 1 hour, then use a knife to gently release the cakes from the sides of the pans. Flip the pans over to release the cakes. Remove the parchment and cool completely, right side up, before frosting.

make it ahead The cake can be made up to 3 days in advance. Wrap each layer in parchment paper first, then tightly with plastic wrap and store in the refrigerator. Bring to room temperature before frosting.

tidbits The batter can be baked in one 9-inch pan for 30 to 35 minutes or in a 12-cavity muffin pan lined with paper cupcake liners for 20 to 25 minutes.

Cut each cake layer in half horizontally for a four-layer cake, frosting between the layers and on the outside and top of the cake, or simply frost between the two layers and stack for a two-layer cake.

red velvet cake

Beet powder and the red color that results when natural cocoa powder is mixed with an acidic ingredient give this cake a naturally red tint (pictured on page 150). It uses a combination of arrowroot and coconut flours to make it nut-free. Try the Cream Cheese Frosting (page 163) for a classic rendition, or for a dairy-free version, use the Dairy-Free Cream Cheese Frosting variation of the Vanilla Buttercream (page 160).

SERVES 8

½ cup palm shortening

½ cup coconut flour

½ cup arrowroot powder

¼ cup plus 2 tablespoons beet powder

¼ cup natural cocoa powder

½ teaspoon grain-free baking powder (page 325)

¼ teaspoon fine sea salt

4 eggs, separated and at room temperature

1 teaspoon cream of tartar

¾ cup light-colored raw honey

½ cup coconut sugar

2 teaspoons freshly squeezed lemon juice

1 teaspoon pure vanilla extract

¼ cup full-fat coconut milk

Melt the palm shortening in a small saucepan set over low heat. Set aside to cool.

Preheat the oven to 350°F. Lightly grease two 6 by 3-inch cake pans with palm shortening and place a round piece of parchment paper at the bottom of each pan.

Sift the coconut flour, arrowroot powder, beet powder, cocoa powder, baking powder, and salt into a large bowl and set aside.

In the bowl of a stand mixer fitted with the whisk attachment, or using an electric handheld mixer, beat the egg whites on medium-high speed for 3 to 5 minutes, until they have tripled in volume and form soft peaks when the whisk is pulled out of the bowl. Add the cream of tartar and beat for another 30 seconds, then scoop the whites into a bowl and set aside.

Return the bowl to the mixer and switch to the beater attachment. Beat together the cooled palm shortening, honey, coconut sugar, lemon juice, and vanilla on medium-high speed for 30 seconds. Add the coconut milk and egg yolks and beat until combined. Gradually add the sifted dry ingredients, mixing after each addition, until fully incorporated. Scrape down the sides of the bowl and along the bottom if necessary and beat again for 30 seconds on high. Gently fold in the beaten egg whites until they are fully incorporated and there are no visible ribbons of whites throughout the batter. Divide the batter between the two pans.

Bake for 30 to 35 minutes, until a toothpick inserted into the center of the cakes comes out clean.

CONTINUED

red velvet cake, continued

Cool the cakes on a wire rack for 30 minutes, then use a knife to gently release the cakes from the sides of the pans. Flip the pans over to release the cakes. Remove the parchment and cool completely, right side up, before frosting.

make it ahead The cake can be made up to 3 days in advance. Wrap the layers in parchment paper first, then tightly with plastic wrap and store in the refrigerator. Bring to room temperature before frosting.

tidbits Beet powder can be found at most health food stores as well as through online retailers such as Nuts.com or Amazon.

Using natural cocoa powder helps to color this cake red. Dutch-processed, or alkalized, cocoa will make it a deeper brownish red.

See Tidbits on page 152 for how to bake one 9-inch cake or 12 cupcakes.

nut-free yellow cake

This cake is a classic option for anyone allergic to nuts. Frost this classic cake with any of the frosting recipes at the end of this chapter. My favorite is a center layer of Raspberry Buttercream (page 160) with an outside frosting of Vanilla Buttercream (page 160).

SERVES 8

4 eggs, separated and at room temperature

⅓ cup palm shortening, softened

½ cup light-colored raw honey

¼ cup pure maple syrup

2 teaspoons pure vanilla extract

1½ teaspoons freshly squeezed lemon juice

3 egg yolks, at room temperature

¾ cup coconut flour

¾ teaspoon baking soda

½ teaspoon fine sea salt

Preheat the oven to 325°F. Lightly grease two 6 by 3-inch cake pans with palm shortening and place a round piece of parchment paper at the bottom of each pan.

In the bowl of a stand mixer fitted with the whisk attachment, or using an electric handheld mixer, beat the 4 egg whites on medium-high speed for 3 to 5 minutes, until they have tripled in volume and form soft peaks when the whisk is pulled out. Scoop the whites into a bowl and set aside.

Return the bowl to the mixer and switch to the beater attachment. Beat together the palm shortening, honey, maple syrup, vanilla, and lemon juice on medium-high speed for 1 minute. Add the 7 yolks and beat again for 30 seconds. Add the coconut flour, baking soda, and salt and beat again for 30 seconds, or until well incorporated. Gently fold in the beaten egg whites until they are fully incorporated and there are no visible ribbons of whites throughout the batter. Divide the batter between the two pans.

Bake for 25 to 30 minutes, until a toothpick inserted into the center of the cakes comes out clean.

Cool the cakes on a wire rack for 1 hour, then use a knife to gently release the cakes from the sides of the pans. Flip the pans over to release the cakes. Remove the parchment and cool completely, right side up, before frosting.

make it ahead The cake can be made up to 3 days in advance. Wrap each layer in parchment paper first, then tightly with plastic wrap and store in the refrigerator. Bring to room temperature before frosting.

tidbits The color of the honey used will dictate the color of this cake. I suggest using a light-colored, mild-flavored raw honey, such as clover.

See Tidbits on page 152 for how to bake one 9-inch cake or 12 cupcakes.

yellow cake

I use a combination of whole eggs and rich yolks as well as golden ghee to achieve the cake's well-known yellow color and buttery flavor (pictured on page 150). Grass-fed unsalted butter or palm shortening is a suitable substitute but will change the color slightly. Frost this classic cake with Chocolate Buttercream (page 160) or Quick Chocolate Icing (page 163).

SERVES 8

3 eggs, separated and at room temperature

¼ cup ghee (page 325), softened

½ cup light-colored raw honey

¼ cup pure maple syrup

1½ teaspoons pure vanilla extract

1 teaspoon freshly squeezed lemon juice

3 egg yolks, at room temperature

1½ cups blanched almond flour

¼ cup arrowroot powder

2 tablespoons coconut flour

½ teaspoon baking soda

¼ teaspoon fine sea salt

Preheat the oven to 325°F. Lightly grease two 6 by 3-inch cake pans with palm shortening and place a round piece of parchment paper at the bottom of each pan.

In the bowl of a stand mixer fitted with the whisk attachment, or using an electric handheld mixer, beat the 3 egg whites on medium-high speed for 3 to 5 minutes, until they have tripled in volume and form soft peaks when the whisk is pulled out. Scoop the whites into a bowl and set aside.

Return the bowl to the mixer and switch to the beater attachment. Beat together the ghee, honey, maple syrup, vanilla, and lemon juice on medium-high speed for 1 minute. Add the 6 yolks and beat again for 30 seconds. Add the almond flour, arrowroot, coconut flour, baking soda, and salt and beat again for 30 seconds, until well incorporated. Gently fold in the beaten egg whites until they are fully incorporated and there are no visible ribbons of whites throughout the batter. Divide the batter between the two pans and gently smooth the tops.

Bake for 30 minutes, or until a toothpick inserted into the center of the cakes comes out clean.

Cool the cakes on a wire rack for 1 hour, then use a knife to gently release the cakes from the sides of the pans. Flip the pans over to release the cakes. Remove the parchment and cool completely, right side up, before frosting.

make it ahead The cake can be made up to 3 days in advance. Wrap each layer in parchment paper first, then tightly with plastic wrap and store in the refrigerator. Bring to room temperature before frosting.

tidbits The color of the honey used will dictate the color of this cake. I suggest using a light-colored, mild-flavored raw honey such as clover.

See Tidbits on page 152 for how to bake one 9-inch cake or 12 cupcakes.

strawberry cake

This light and fruity cake (pictured on page 151) tastes delicious with a layer of Raspberry Buttercream (page 160) in the center and frosted with either the Vanilla Buttercream (page 160) or Cream Cheese Frosting (page 163).

SERVES 8

⅓ cup coconut oil, melted

4 eggs, at room temperature

2½ cups blanched almond flour

½ cup light-colored raw honey

1 tablespoon freshly squeezed lemon juice

2 teaspoons pure vanilla extract

¾ teaspoon baking soda

¼ teaspoon fine sea salt

½ cup chopped strawberries

½ teaspoon finely grated lemon zest

Preheat the oven to 325°F. Lightly grease two 6 by 3-inch cake pans with palm shortening and place a round piece of parchment paper at the bottom of each pan.

Combine the coconut oil, eggs, almond flour, honey, lemon juice, and vanilla in a food processor. Process for 45 seconds, until smooth. If necessary, scrape down the sides and process again. Add the baking soda and salt and process for 15 seconds, to create a smooth batter. Fold in the strawberries and lemon zest. Divide the batter evenly between the prepared pans.

Bake for 30 to 35 minutes, until a toothpick inserted into the center of the cakes comes out clean.

Cool the cakes on a wire rack for 20 minutes, then use a knife to gently release the cakes from the sides of the pans. Flip the pans over to release the cakes. Remove the parchment and cool completely, right side up, before frosting.

make it ahead The cake can be made up to 3 days in advance. Wrap each layer in parchment paper first, then tightly with plastic wrap and store in the refrigerator. Bring to room temperature before frosting.

tidbits See Tidbits on page 152 for how to bake one 9-inch cake or 12 cupcakes.

vanilla cake

This white cake is light and works wonderfully as the base for any of your vanilla cake needs. Our favorite way to eat it is with a layer of raspberry jam in the center and Raspberry Buttercream (page 160) on the outside.

(page 160)

SERVES 8

5 egg whites, at room temperature

¼ cup full-fat coconut milk

¼ cup palm shortening, softened

¼ cup light-colored raw honey

¼ cup pure maple syrup

2 teaspoons pure vanilla extract

½ teaspoon freshly squeezed lemon juice

1½ cups blanched almond flour

3 tablespoons arrowroot powder

3 tablespoons coconut flour

½ teaspoon baking soda

Preheat the oven to 325°F. Lightly grease two 6 by 3-inch cake pans with palm shortening and place a round piece of parchment paper at the bottom of each pan.

In the bowl of a stand mixer fitted with the whisk attachment, or using an electric handheld mixer, beat the egg whites on medium-high speed for 3 to 5 minutes, until they have tripled in volume and form soft peaks when the whisk is pulled out. Scoop the whites into a bowl and set aside. Return the bowl to the mixer and switch to the beater attachment. Beat together the coconut milk, palm shortening, honey, maple syrup, vanilla, and lemon juice on medium-high speed for 30 seconds. Add the almond flour, arrowroot, coconut flour, and baking soda and beat again for 30 seconds, or until well incorporated. Gently fold in the beaten egg whites with a rubber spatula until they are fully incorporated and there are no visible ribbons of whites throughout the batter. Divide the batter between the two pans.

Bake the cake for 30 minutes, or until a toothpick inserted into the center of the cakes comes out clean.

Cool the cakes on a wire rack for 1 hour, then use a knife to gently release the cakes from the sides of the pans. Flip the pans over to release the cakes. Remove the parchment and cool completely, right side, up before frosting.

make it ahead The cake can be made up to 3 days in advance. Wrap the layers in parchment paper first, then tightly with plastic wrap and store in the refrigerator. Bring to room temperature before frosting.

tidbits The color of the honey used will dictate the color of this cake. I suggest using a light-colored, mild-flavored raw honey, such as clover.

See Tidbits on page 152 for how to bake one 9-inch cake or 12 cupcakes.

See Tidbits on page 152 for how to bake one 9-inch cake or 12 cupcakes.

vanilla buttercream

A lot of Paleo versions of buttercream are bland and must be refrigerated to hold a firm texture. I created this one to be egg-free, and it's beautifully creamy and firm from the gelatin that is used, even at room temperature.

MAKES 2 CUPS

1 cup water

4½ teaspoons unflavored gelatin powder

1 cup light-colored raw honey

2 teaspoons pure vanilla extract

2 cups palm shortening, softened (see Tidbits, page 162)

6 tablespoons arrowroot powder

Pinch of fine sea salt

Place ½ cup of the water in the bowl of a stand mixer fitted with the whisk attachment and sprinkle the gelatin over it. Allow to bloom, or absorb the water, for 10 minutes.

Combine the remaining ½ cup water and the honey in a saucepan and bring to a boil over medium-high heat. Simmer for 12 to 15 minutes, swirling occasionally, until a candy thermometer reads 240°F.

Turn the mixer on low, and with it running, slowly pour the hot honey syrup down the side of the bowl. Once it is all poured in, increase the speed of the mixer to medium-high and beat for 8 to 10 minutes, until the mixture and the outside of the bowl are at room temperature. The mixture will turn from brown to white and triple in volume.

Add the vanilla, palm shortening, arrowroot, and salt and beat on low until combined. Then beat on medium-high speed for 3 minutes, or until cooled and smooth.

The frosting can be used immediately, or, for easier piping, place the frosting in the refrigerator for 1 hour, or until set.

VARIATIONS

Chocolate Buttercream Gently melt 6 ounces of dark chocolate (at least 85 percent cacao) and let it cool to room temperature. Fold it into the frosting prior to refrigerating.

Raspberry Buttercream Puree and strain the seeds from 2 cups of raspberries and fold into the frosting prior to refrigerating.

Dairy-Free Cream Cheese Frosting Mix 2 teaspoons raw tahini and 2 teaspoons freshly squeezed lemon juice into the frosting prior to refrigerating.

CONTINUED

Clockwise from top: chocolate buttercream, raspberry buttercream, quick chocolate icing, cream cheese frosting, and vanilla buttercream

vanilla buttercream, continued

tidbits Tropical Traditions brand palm shortening or grass-fed unsalted butter works best with this recipe. Certain store-bought brands contain oils other than pure palm shortening and may make this frosting too runny. If the frosting turns out too runny, beat in additional palm shortening, 1 tablespoon at a time, until it comes together. For Spectrum brand shortening, use 2½ cups shortening and beat in 2 tablespoons pure maple syrup before refrigerating.

The frosting will hold up at room temperature (around 70°F) for a few hours but is easier to pipe when chilled. When mixing, if the frosting starts to look curdled, it is likely the gelatin mixture was not sufficiently cooled when the palm shortening was added, or the palm shortening was too warm when added. Put the bowl in the refrigerator for 20 minutes, then resume beating until smooth. If the frosting is still curdled, beat in additional palm shortening, 1 tablespoon at a time, until smooth.

The color of the honey used will dictate the color of this frosting. I suggest using a light colored, mild-flavored raw honey, such as clover.

cream cheese frosting

This frosting (pictured on page 161) has goat dairy in it, but I just could not put out a celebrations book without a form of cream cheese frosting to use on my Carrot Cake (page 102) or Red Velvet Cake (page 153). Can't do dairy? Try the Dairy-Free Cream Cheese Frosting variation of the Vanilla Buttercream on page 160.

MAKES 2 CUPS

8 ounces chèvre (soft fresh goat cheese), chilled

½ cup light-colored raw honey

¼ cup coconut butter, softened

3 tablespoons palm shortening, softened

1½ teaspoons pure vanilla extract

In the bowl of a stand mixer fitted with the whisk attachment, or using an electric handheld mixer, beat the cheese for 1 minute on medium-high speed. Add the honey, coconut butter, palm shortening, and vanilla and continue beating for 1 minute, or until smooth and creamy. If the frosting is too thin, refrigerate for 1 hour before frosting cakes or cupcakes.

tidbit Coconut butter becomes very solid if chilled. To soften, place the jar in a bowl of hot water for 5 to 10 minutes, until it is soft enough to easily stir.

quick chocolate icing

This quick icing (pictured on page 161) has a deep chocolate flavor and is perfect for spreading atop cupcakes or frosting a simple cake.

MAKES 3 CUPS

2 cups palm shortening or grass-fed unsalted butter, softened

1 cup pure maple syrup

1 tablespoon pure vanilla extract

1 cup natural cocoa powder

¾ cup arrowroot powder

½ teaspoon fine sea salt

In the bowl of a stand mixer fitted with the whisk attachment, or using an electric handheld mixer, beat the palm shortening on medium-high speed for 30 seconds. Add the maple syrup and vanilla and beat again for 30 seconds, or until combined. Add the cocoa powder, arrowroot, and salt and beat on low speed until incorporated, then beat on medium-high speed for 30 seconds.

Spread the icing on cooled cakes or cupcakes, or place in the refrigerator to thicken for piping. Store in the refrigerator for up to 1 week. Bring to room temperature and beat briefly with the beater attachment or a handheld electric mixer until smooth before spreading onto cakes.

Fourth of July
barbecue

Where I grew up, we had a neighborhood block party every year on Independence Day. Everyone contributed to a big potluck, the grills were fired up in the front yards, and fireworks were set off in the street for the children's amusement before the big night sky show began. I remember decorating my bike every year to ride in a parade and gathering with friends and family in the evening to eat burgers, watermelon, potato salad, and ice-cold sodas. I have so many fond memories of those summer gatherings.

A backyard barbecue is one of my favorites to host because it can be effortless in the planning and decor department and just focus on fun, seasonal food, and dining under the stars. Just put some wildflowers in mason jars around the table, string some twinkling lights between the trees, and let the food be the star. These recipes can be used for any of your summer events, including Memorial Day, Labor Day, or just a family dinner alfresco.

I've included my all-time favorite hamburger recipe in this chapter (it's topped with BLT ingredients, so what's not to love?), which you can serve either on a grain-free bun or simply wrapped in lettuce, as well as a new rendition of the most adored salmon recipe from my blog. Make both recipes to give your guests a barbecue surf-and-turf combination, or choose one or the other. My grandmother's recipe for a slightly nontraditional potato salad and a berry tart with a creamy vanilla-custard filling combine with both of the main dishes for a complete and festive meal. Wash it all down with homemade ice-cold ginger ale and let the memories of childhood summers roll on in.

Happy Fourth!

heirloom tomato, watermelon, and basil salad

This dish is simple to prepare and combines many quintessential summer flavors in one fresh salad. Although a colorful array of heirloom tomatoes is simply stunning in this salad, any flavorful vine-ripened tomatoes would be wonderful when heirlooms are not available.

SERVES 8

1 small (3- to 4-pound) seedless watermelon

2 pounds heirloom tomatoes

2 Kirby or other pickling cucumber

3 tablespoons extra-virgin olive oil

1 tablespoon champagne vinegar

½ cup chopped fresh basil

Fine sea salt

Cut away the rind from the watermelon, then cut it into 1-inch-wide wedges. Slice the tomatoes and cucumbers into thin rounds. Toss the watermelon, tomatoes, cucumbers, olive oil, vinegar, and basil together in a wide bowl. Season with salt. Place the bowl in the refrigerator for 2 hours, then serve chilled.

tidbits An almond-based ricotta cheese substitute, such as the recipe from my first cookbook, *Against All Grain,* or from Kite Hill brand (available at Whole Foods), tastes delicious sprinkled over this salad.

grandma's potato salad

I love to use white sweet potatoes, like the Hannah variety, in my potato salad for a touch of sweetness and for the bounty of nutrients present in a sweet potato versus an Irish potato. Every summer, my grandma Bonnie would make this salad for family gatherings, and whenever I make it now, it brings back warm memories of those get-togethers.

SERVES 8

2 pounds Hannah sweet potatoes or other white-fleshed variety, peeled and cubed

½ cup mayonnaise (page 328)

¼ cup full-fat coconut milk

¼ cup chopped fresh dill

1 tablespoon apple cider vinegar

2 teaspoons prepared yellow mustard

1¾ teaspoons fine sea salt

½ teaspoon sweet paprika

½ cup peeled and diced cucumber

¼ cup cherry tomatoes, halved

¼ cup diced celery

Put the sweet potatoes in a large pot, fill with water, and add a generous pinch of salt. Bring to a boil and cook for 8 minutes, or until the potatoes are fork-tender. Drain and let cool.

In a large mixing bowl, whisk together the mayonnaise, coconut milk, dill, vinegar, mustard, salt, and paprika. Fold in the cooled potatoes, cucumber, tomatoes, and celery. Cover and chill overnight. Serve cold.

make it ahead This potato salad gets better with time! The flavors are at their fullest after 24 hours in the refrigerator, and it will keep for up to 5 days.

blta burger with special sauce

A standard BLT sandwich is kicked up a notch by adding a juicy grass-fed burger, special sauce, and grilled tomatoes and avocados. This is my family's favorite burger to eat all summer long. Serve it on a lettuce wrap or on a grain-free roll.

special sauce

¼ cup mayonnaise
(page 328)

2 tablespoons ketchup
(page 328)

1 tablespoon chopped
dill pickles

1 teaspoon apple cider
vinegar

burgers

3 pounds ground grass-fed
beef

¼ cup grated yellow onion

3 tablespoons extra-virgin
olive oil

1 tablespoon prepared
yellow mustard

½ teaspoon fine sea salt

¼ teaspoon freshly ground
black pepper

blta salsa

8 slices thick-cut bacon

2 tomatoes, diced

2 avocados, pitted, peeled,
and diced

Fine sea salt and freshly
ground black pepper

8 poppy seed hamburger
buns (page 330) or lettuce,
for serving

1 head iceberg lettuce,
finely shredded

To make the special sauce, combine the mayonnaise, ketchup, pickles, and vinegar in a bowl and mix well. Cover and place in the refrigerator until you're ready to serve.

To make the burgers, gently mix together the beef, onion, olive oil, mustard, salt, and pepper in a bowl. Use your hands to loosely form eight 3-inch patties. Preheat a grill for indirect-heat cooking to medium-high heat.

To make the BLTA salsa, in a large skillet, fry the bacon over medium heat, flipping the bacon once, until crisp, about 8 minutes. Remove from the pan and let cool on a plate lined with a paper towel. Combine the tomatoes and avocados in a bowl and season with salt and pepper. Dice the bacon and add it to the bowl.

Sear the patties over direct heat for 2 minutes on each side. Move the patties to indirect heat as far from the coals or gas jets as possible and cook for 5 minutes more per side, or until a meat thermometer reads 160°F for medium doneness. Remove the burgers from the grill and tent with aluminum foil to keep warm.

Serve each burger on a bun with the BLTA salsa, shredded lettuce, and special sauce.

make it ahead Make the sauce and store it in the refrigerator for up to 5 days. Form the patties and place them on a baking sheet with parchment paper between the layers. Cover tightly and refrigerate for up to 2 days or freeze for up to 3 months. Defrost in the refrigerator overnight and bring to room temperature before grilling.

tidbits Grass-fed beef is leaner than conventionally raised beef, which can lead to dry burgers. The onions and olive oil in the patties help to add moisture, and forming thick patties loosely helps to prevent dryness.

blackened salmon with stone-fruit salsa

Seasoned salmon served with a vibrant and bold-flavored salsa of summer fruits makes this dish a crowd-pleaser at every barbecue. I always opt for fresh wild salmon rather than frozen and farmed. When it goes on sale at my local market, or when I occasionally see it at my Costco store, I buy a few extra fillets and freeze them for later use.

SERVES 8

salsa

1 large avocado, pitted, peeled, and diced

1 Pluot, pitted and diced

1 large yellow nectarine, pitted and diced

1 large yellow peach, pitted and diced

1 jalapeño chile, seeded and minced

2 tablespoons minced red onion

1 teaspoon freshly squeezed lime juice

½ teaspoon fine sea salt

2 tablespoons chopped fresh cilantro

1 tablespoon extra-virgin olive oil

2 cloves garlic, crushed

2 tablespoons blackening seasoning (page 323)

2 pounds wild salmon fillet, skin on

To make the salsa, combine the avocado, Pluot, nectarine, peach, jalapeño, red onion, lime juice, and salt in a bowl. Refrigerate until you are ready to serve.

Preheat a grill for indirect-heat cooking to medium-high heat.

Combine the olive oil, garlic, and blackening seasoning in a bowl. Rub the mixture over both sides of the salmon and leave the salmon at room temperature while the grill heats.

Place the salmon, skin side down, over direct heat on the grill and close the grill lid. Cook for 1 to 3 minutes on the first side, depending on the thickness. Do not move the salmon until it releases easily. Using tongs in one hand and a metal spatula in the other, carefully turn the fish over so the skin side is up and the fish is over the coolest part of the grill. Close the grill lid and finish cooking over indirect heat for about 5 minutes more, depending on the thickness of the fillet. The salmon is ready when it is just barely opaque and starts to flake along the center of the fillet.

To serve, fold the cilantro into the fruit salsa. Serve the salmon hot with the salsa spooned over it.

make it ahead Make the salsa, without the avocado and cilantro, up to 3 days in advance and store it in an airtight container in the refrigerator. Stir in the avocado and cilantro just prior to serving. Rub the salmon with the seasoning 1 day before grilling and wrap tightly before storing in the refrigerator.

tidbits The rub and salsa both taste delicious on chicken if wild salmon is not available or affordable in your area.

berry tart with vanilla bean custard

Vibrant berries are in abundance at farmers' markets during the summer months, and this tart with creamy vanilla bean custard and a nut-free shortbread crust showcases them perfectly.

SERVES 8

custard filling

1¾ teaspoons unflavored gelatin powder

1 tablespoon water

1 cup almond milk (page 320), or coconut milk (for nut-free)

1 vanilla bean, seeds scraped and bean reserved

3 egg yolks

¼ cup light-colored raw honey

2 (13.5-ounce) cans full-fat coconut milk, refrigerated for at least 24 hours

crust

¾ cup coconut flour

½ cup arrowroot powder

½ cup palm shortening, ghee (page 325), or coconut oil

¼ cup maple sugar

½ teaspoon pure vanilla extract

½ teaspoon fine sea salt

2 eggs

3 cups mixed fresh berries

Edible flowers, for garnish (optional)

To make the filling, soften the gelatin by placing it in a bowl with the water. In a saucepan, heat the almond milk and vanilla bean seeds and pod over medium-high heat for 2 to 3 minutes, until heated through. Whisk the egg yolks and honey in a bowl, then slowly add the milk mixture while whisking constantly to temper the egg yolks. Return the mixture to the pan and heat for 2 to 3 minutes while whisking constantly, until heated through but not boiling. Whisk in the softened gelatin until it dissolves completely. Cook for 5 minutes more, or until the custard has thickened and coats the back of a spoon. Pour the custard through a fine-mesh sieve into a bowl and press a piece of plastic wrap directly on top to prevent a skin from forming. Refrigerate until set, at least 5 hours.

Preheat the oven to 350°F. To make the crust, in the bowl of a stand mixer fitted with the beater attachment, or using a handheld electric mixer, combine the coconut flour, arrowroot, palm shortening, maple sugar, vanilla, and salt. Mix on medium speed to combine. Add the eggs and beat on medium-high until a loose dough forms. Press the dough into the bottom and up the sides of a 9-inch tart pan with a removable base. Cut a circle of parchment paper and lightly press it onto the bottom of the crust. Fill with pie weights or dried beans, then bake for 10 minutes. Remove the weights and parchment, bake for 5 minutes more, then cool.

Carefully open the chilled cans of coconut milk and spoon off enough thick cream from the tops to total 1 cup. Pour the cream into the custard. Reserve the remaining coconut milk for another use.

Add the custard to the bowl of a stand mixer fitted with the whisk attachment, or use a handheld electric mixer, and whip the custard until creamy. Spread the custard in the cooled crust, then chill for 2 hours, or until set. Remove the pan sides, then arrange the berries and flowers on top of the filling and serve immediately.

make it ahead Bake the crust up to 2 days in advance and store, tightly wrapped, in the refrigerator. The custard will keep for up to 4 days, stored separately from the crust.

ginger ale

Ice-cold ginger ale has always been one of my favorite beverages for a summertime barbecue, but it is usually made with refined sugar or high-fructose corn syrup. The ginger flavor in commercial brands is also quite mild, and I really like a ginger-packed drink. So I started making ginger ale at home. Homemade soda is easier to make than you probably think, and you can store the syrup without the carbonated water for up to a week.

SERVES 8

ginger syrup

8 ounces fresh ginger, peeled and chopped

8 cups water

2 cups light-colored raw honey

8 cups sparkling water

4 tablespoons freshly squeezed lemon or lime juice

Ice, for serving

To make the syrup, combine the ginger and water in a saucepan and bring to a boil. Turn down the heat to low and simmer for 45 minutes, or until the liquid has reduced by half. Remove from the heat and stir in the honey. Cover for 20 minutes to let the ginger and honey steep. Strain the ginger out and refrigerate the ginger syrup until well chilled.

In a large pitcher, combine the ginger syrup, sparkling water, and lemon juice and stir well. Serve over ice.

make it ahead Make the syrup up to 1 week in advance and store it in an airtight container in the refrigerator.

tidbits Add muddled fresh fruit such as peaches or berries to dress this drink up and turn it into a party-worthy cocktail!

summer
shower

I can't tell you how many times I've attended a baby or bridal shower and had to either forgo the food completely or pick apart a sandwich to eat only the insides. At these celebratory showers, often held in the summertime, the menu usually involves sweet little tea sandwiches or brunch items like quiche, muffins, and croissants—none of which I can safely eat.

In this chapter, I set out to create a menu for a lovely daytime event that can be used in place of the standard grain-filled dishes. These small bites—including four variations of deviled eggs (the smoked salmon and truffled bacon versions are amazing) and California-style marinated ahi tuna tartar served on crisp root chips with cool cucumber and avocado—are some of my favorite special-occasion recipes. They are just so fresh and satisfying. And watch out: the fragrant mini Bundt cakes may just become a summertime staple.

These items will shower a grain-free bride or mom-to-be with love, and I guarantee that guests who do not have any food restrictions will enjoy them every bit as much. This menu can also be a wonderful option for another celebration, such as an adult's birthday party (the children's birthday party menu is on page 139), Mother's Day, or a graduation brunch.

Congratulations to the blushing bride or momma-to-be!

From top: smoked salmon, pesto,
truffled bacon, and avocado tarragon

deviled eggs, four ways

It's so hard to choose just one style of deviled egg, so I've given you four of my favorite fillings from which to pick and choose. If you're feeling really ambitious, make them all and let your shower guests have some variety.

SERVES 12

12 eggs

smoked salmon filling

12 hard-boiled egg yolks

⅓ cup mayonnaise (page 328)

¼ cup full-fat coconut milk

1 tablespoon finely chopped fresh dill

1 tablespoon finely chopped fresh flat-leaf parsley

¾ teaspoon Dijon mustard

¾ teaspoon finely chopped fresh chives

½ teaspoon onion powder

½ teaspoon fine sea salt

3 ounces smoked salmon, thinly sliced, for garnish

1 tablespoon capers, for garnish

pesto filling

12 hard-boiled egg yolks

⅓ cup store-bought dairy-free pesto sauce

½ cup extra-virgin olive oil

2½ teaspoons freshly squeezed lemon juice

3 tablespoons chopped sun-dried tomatoes, for garnish

3 tablespoons lightly toasted pine nuts, for garnish

To prepare the eggs, place 12 eggs in a single layer in a large saucepan and add water to cover by at least 2 inches. Heat over high heat until the water begins to boil, then cover and turn off the heat. Let the eggs sit for 10 minutes, then drain and rinse the eggs under cold water for 1 minute. Crack the eggshells and carefully peel under cool running water. Dry the outsides and slice the eggs in half lengthwise. Put the yolks in a bowl and set aside for the filling. Place the whites on a serving platter, cover with plastic wrap, and refrigerate until ready to fill.

Make the filling of your choice and fill and garnish the eggs as directed. Cover and refrigerate the deviled eggs until ready to serve.

To make the smoked salmon filling, combine the reserved hard-boiled egg yolks, the mayonnaise, coconut milk, dill, parsley, mustard, chives, onion powder, and salt in a bowl. Mash the mixture until well combined and smooth. Spoon the mixture into a large zip-top bag and snip off a hole in the bottom corner. Pipe the mixture into the egg whites and garnish with the smoked salmon and capers.

To make the pesto filling, combine the reserved hard-boiled egg yolks, the pesto sauce, olive oil, and lemon juice in a bowl. Mash the mixture until well combined and smooth. Spoon the mixture into a large zip-top bag and snip off a hole in the bottom corner. Pipe the mixture into the egg whites and garnish with the sun-dried tomatoes and pine nuts.

CONTINUED

deviled eggs, four ways, continued

avocado tarragon filling

12 hard-boiled egg yolks

2 avocados, pitted

3 cloves garlic, minced

2 tablespoons freshly squeezed lemon juice

1 tablespoon avocado oil

2 teaspoons finely chopped fresh tarragon

1½ teaspoons white wine vinegar

1½ teaspoons Dijon mustard

½ teaspoon fine sea salt

¼ cup microgreens, for garnish

truffled bacon filling

8 slices bacon

12 hard-boiled egg yolks

⅓ cup mayonnaise (page 328)

3 tablespoons Dijon mustard

2 tablespoons chopped fresh chives

½ teaspoon white truffle oil

¼ teaspoon fine sea salt

½ teaspoon sweet paprika or cayenne pepper, for garnish

To make the avocado tarragon filling, combine the reserved hard-boiled egg yolks, the flesh of the avocados, garlic, lemon juice, avocado oil, tarragon, vinegar, mustard, and salt in a bowl. Mash the mixture until well combined and smooth. Spoon the mixture into a large zip-top bag and snip off a hole in the bottom corner. Pipe the mixture into the egg whites and garnish with the microgreens.

To make the truffled bacon filling, cook the bacon in a large cast-iron skillet over medium heat, flipping once, until crisp, about 8 minutes. Remove the bacon from the pan and drain it on a plate lined with paper towels, then coarsely chop. Combine the reserved hard-boiled egg yolks, mayonnaise, mustard, chives, truffle oil, and salt in a bowl. Mash the mixture until well combined and smooth. Spoon the mixture into a large zip-top bag and snip off a hole in the bottom corner. Pipe the mixture into the egg whites and garnish with the chopped bacon and a sprinkle of paprika.

make it ahead All of these variations can be made up to 2 days in advance, except for the avocado variation, which should be served immediately. Fill the eggs and store them on a platter, wrapped tightly with plastic wrap, in the refrigerator. Serve chilled.

tidbits To get super smooth deviled egg filling, use an immersion blender to blend the mixture.

ahi tartare on taro chips

I would eat ahi tartare or poke every day if I could. In this simple appetizer, fresh ahi, cool avocado, and crunchy cucumber and radishes are tossed in a citrus-ginger marinade and piled on top of crisp taro chips. I love to combine any leftovers with the chips for a quick and fresh lunch.

SERVES 10

2 pounds skinless fillet ahi tuna

½ cup freshly squeezed lime juice

⅓ cup coconut aminos

¼ cup freshly squeezed orange juice

¼ cup finely grated orange zest

¼ cup rice vinegar

3 tablespoons peeled and minced fresh ginger

2 cloves garlic, minced

2 teaspoons light-colored raw honey

1½ teaspoons fine sea salt

1 teaspoon dried red pepper flakes

½ cup extra-virgin olive oil

2 Persian cucumbers, diced

6 radishes, thinly sliced

3 avocados, pitted, peeled, and diced

12 ounces store-bought taro chips, for serving

½ cup chopped green onions, tender green and white parts, for garnish

¼ cup black sesame seeds, for garnish

Place the tuna in the freezer for 30 minutes to firm it up, making it easier to dice. Remove it from the freezer and cut it into ¼-inch-thick slices, then cut the slices into ¼-inch cubes.

In a bowl, whisk together the lime juice, coconut aminos, orange juice, orange zest, vinegar, ginger, garlic, honey, salt, and red pepper flakes. Slowly drizzle in the olive oil while continuously whisking.

Stir the tuna, cucumber, and radish into the sauce. Gently fold in the avocado right before serving. Spoon the tartare on top of the taro chips. Garnish with the green onions and sesame seeds and serve.

make it ahead The fresher the better for seafood, but the tuna, cucumber, and radish mixture can be made a day ahead of serving and stored in an airtight container in the refrigerator. Stir in the avocado right before serving.

tidbits Look for taro chips at health food stores. If you feel like making your own, you will find many simple recipes on the Web for homemade taro chips. Also, feel free to substitute sweet potato chips here.

chicken salad biscuits

These chicken salad biscuits are dainty enough to be served at a shower, but hearty and filling, so your guests will leave satisfied. My grandmother always served her chicken salad in lettuce cups, which is another option here.

---

biscuits

3 cups (about 450g) whole raw cashews

6 eggs, separated

1½ teaspoons apple cider vinegar

½ cup almond milk (page 320)

⅔ cup coconut flour

½ cup blanched almond flour

2 teaspoons baking soda

1½ teaspoons fine sea salt

½ cup palm shortening, softened

1 egg, mixed with 1 tablespoon full-fat coconut milk, for wash

chicken salad

1 pound boneless, skinless chicken breasts

Fine sea salt and freshly ground black pepper

½ cup mayonnaise (page 328)

3 tablespoons full-fat coconut milk

¾ cup seedless red grapes, halved

1 green apple, cored and diced

¼ cup diced celery

2 tablespoons each chopped fresh sage and green onion

1 tablespoon freshly squeezed lemon juice

1 tablespoon champagne vinegar

¼ cup each chopped pecans and walnuts, toasted

Preheat the oven to 325°F. Line a baking sheet with parchment paper.

To make the biscuits, process the cashews in a food processor for about 10 seconds, until ground to a fine flour. Add the egg yolks, vinegar, and almond milk and process again for 10 seconds, or until the mixture resembles a thick paste. Add the coconut flour, almond flour, baking soda, and salt and process again.

Beat the egg whites in a bowl by hand or with an electric handheld mixer, until soft peaks form. Add the egg whites and palm shortening to the food processor and pulse 6 to 8 times, until the egg whites are just incorporated. Place a greased 3-inch biscuit cutter on the prepared baking sheet, spoon the dough into it, and then lift away the cutter. Repeat to make 10 mounds, then lightly press the mounds down with your fingers. Brush the biscuits with the egg wash. Bake for 30 minutes, or until golden brown. Cool on a rack.

To make the chicken salad, bring a pot of water to a boil. Add the chicken, season the water generously with salt and pepper, cover, lower the heat to medium-low, and cook for 5 minutes. Remove from the heat and let stand for 10 to 12 minutes, until a thermometer inserted into the chicken reads 160°F. Remove the chicken from the water and let cool completely.

Shred the chicken with two forks in a bowl. Mix with the mayonnaise, coconut milk, grapes, apple, celery, sage, green onion, lemon juice, and vinegar. Season with salt and pepper. Cover and chill for 30 minutes.

Just before serving, stir the nuts into the chicken salad, then cut the biscuits in half and fill with the chicken salad mixture.

make it ahead Bake the biscuits and store in an airtight container in the refrigerator for up to 1 week. Bring to room temperature before slicing and filling. Make the chicken salad the day before and store in an airtight container in the refrigerator.

lemon lavender bundt cakes

With a lovely lavender and lemon flavor, these light and fresh cakes are wonderful to enjoy on a warm summer afternoon. I especially adore the lemon and coconut glaze and the pretty accent of lavender buds sprinkled on top. If I ever have any of these left over after a party, I love to eat one in the morning with a cup of hot tea.

MAKES 12 CAKES

3 cups blanched almond flour

½ cup arrowroot powder

2 tablespoons dried lavender

⅓ cup palm shortening, melted

¾ cup light-colored raw honey

¼ cup almond milk (page 320)

¼ cup freshly squeezed lemon juice

1 tablespoon finely grated lemon zest

1 teaspoon pure vanilla extract

4 eggs, at room temperature

1 teaspoon baking soda

¼ teaspoon fine sea salt

glaze

3 tablespoons light-colored raw honey

1 teaspoon freshly squeezed lemon juice

1 teaspoon dried lavender

½ teaspoon finely grated lemon zest

½ cup coconut butter

¼ cup water

Preheat the oven to 325°F. Grease two 6-cavity mini silicone Bundt pans well with palm shortening and place them on a baking sheet.

Combine the almond flour, arrowroot powder, and lavender in a food processor and process for 15 seconds, or until finely ground. Add the palm shortening, honey, almond milk, lemon juice, lemon zest, and vanilla and process until well combined. Add the eggs, one at a time, blending after each addition until incorporated. Add the baking soda and salt and process again until combined. Pour the batter into the prepared pans.

Bake for 20 to 25 minutes, until a toothpick inserted into the center of the cakes comes out clean. Cool on a wire rack for 15 minutes, then gently release the cakes from the pans and cool completely.

To make the glaze, heat the honey, lemon juice, lavender, and lemon zest in a small saucepan over medium heat. Simmer for 5 minutes, then remove from the heat and whisk in the coconut butter and water until smooth. Dip the top of each cake in the glaze, then place the cakes in the refrigerator for 20 minutes to set. Serve immediately or store the cakes tightly wrapped in the refrigerator for up to 5 days.

tidbits It is important to use a light-colored raw honey, such as clover, so the glaze is white when it hardens.

Look for culinary lavender at specialty food stores, tea and spice shops, or online.

zabaglione with berries

Zabaglione, zabaione, or sabayon is a light custard made with egg yolks, sugar, and a sweet wine. I like to serve it with vibrant berries for a light and sweet ending to a spring menu. An electric handheld mixer will be your friend for this recipe, or prepare for a good arm workout if you're going to do this by hand!

SERVES 10

12 egg yolks

⅔ cup light-colored raw honey

½ cup sweet Marsala or Madeira wine

1 pint strawberries, hulled and sliced or quartered

1 pint raspberries

1 pint blueberries

Combine the egg yolks, honey, and wine in a stainless-steel bowl. Pour water to a depth of 1 inch into a large saucepan and bring to a simmer over medium-low heat. Set the bowl over the saucepan to create a double boiler. Using an electric handheld mixer on medium speed, or a whisk, beat the mixture until it is warm, holds a ribbon, and resembles a light pudding, 7 to 10 minutes. Be careful not to let the water boil or the yolks will curdle. Set aside to cool slightly.

To serve, put the berries into the bottom of glasses or desserts bowls and top with the warm zabaglione.

make it ahead This custard is best served immediately; however, you can stir 1 cup whipped coconut cream (page 331) into the cooled zabaglione for stability and store in an airtight container in the refrigerator for 2 days, if desired.

mimosa bar

Toast the bride or mom-to-be with these fruity mimosas made with chilled Champagne, sweet fruit juice, and a garnish of fresh fruit. (Of course, serve the mom-to-be herself a pregnancy-friendly mocktail using sparkling water instead of Champagne.)

SERVES 12

3 (750-ml) bottles Champagne or Prosecco (see Tidbits)

Assorted 100 percent fruit juices, such as cherry, grapefruit, or orange

Fresh berries and diced fruits, for the glasses

To set up the mimosa bar, open one bottle of Champagne and place it with the two unopened bottles in ice buckets filled with ice to keep the Champagne cold. Pour the fruit juices into separate clear glass pitchers or bottles and arrange the fruits on a platter to coordinate with the juices. Set out champagne flutes or other stemmed glassware. Invite guests to fill the flutes with equal amounts of Champagne and a fruit juice of their choice and to garnish with the fresh fruit.

tidbits Naturally flavored unsweetened sparkling water, such as one of the more than one dozen flavors offered by LaCroix, makes a great Champagne substitute for a nonalcoholic version.

halloween

trick or treats

Each year on Halloween, my mom invited all of our neighbors and friends over for a big dinner to nourish the kids before letting us loose to collect our loot bags of sugar. This was a tradition she carried on from my grandmother, and I always looked forward to it.

Since most grain-free kids cannot eat a lot of the traditional treats served at Halloween, I've created a spread of festive and spooky foods for little ones to enjoy. For something sweet, they can munch on spider-themed cookies, my take on peanut-butter cups, or creepy crawly gummy worms buried in a chocolate pudding with chocolate cookie "dirt." For kids who prefer savory flavors, there's a warm mummy dog they'll love to dip in ketchup or mustard. Make all or just some of the festive foods in this chapter, and serve them buffet-style for the kids to snack on before going trick-or-treating.

Just like my siblings and I did as kids at the end of the night, Asher comes home and sorts through his candy while sitting on the floor. I let him pick a few special pieces, and he trades the rest for my homemade items, a gift card to pick out a small toy, or natural, dye-free candies that I find at the health food store.

Happy Halloween!

menu

◆◆◆

Spider Cookies

Dirt Cups

Sunbutter Chocolate Cups

Caramel-Filled Chocolate Candies

Caramel Apples

Mummy Dogs

Witches' Fingers

spider cookies

These cookies are similar to a peanut butter blossom cookie but with a creepy-crawly twist! Instead of peanut butter, which is in the legume family, I use sunflower seed butter to keep these treats both Paleo and nut-free. I've also made them egg-free, so your little ones with allergies can choose the treat instead of the trick.

MAKES 12 COOKIES

3 tablespoons palm shortening or grass-fed unsalted butter

¼ cup unsweetened sunflower seed butter, chilled

3 tablespoons light-colored raw honey

⅓ cup coconut sugar

2 teaspoons pure vanilla extract

1 teaspoon freshly squeezed lemon juice

¼ cup plus 2 tablespoons coconut flour

¼ teaspoon baking soda

2 ounces dark chocolate (85 percent cacao), chopped

Preheat the oven to 350°F. Line a baking sheet with parchment paper.

In a stand mixer fitted with the beater attachment, or using an electric handheld beater, cream together the palm shortening and sunflower butter for 30 seconds, or until light and creamy. Keep the mixer running and add the honey, coconut sugar, vanilla, and lemon juice. Turn the mixer off and add the coconut flour and baking soda. Beat on high for 30 seconds until combined. Let the dough sit for 5 minutes, then beat again on high for 15 seconds. Roll balls of dough slightly smaller than golf balls between your palms and place them on the prepared baking sheet spaced ½ inch apart.

Bake for 12 minutes, or until lightly browned around the edges. When the cookies come out of the oven, lightly indent the tops with your fingertip. Cool completely on a wire rack.

Gently melt the chocolate in the top of a double boiler. Let it cool until it is at room temperature and thick enough to hold its shape when piped. Spoon the chocolate into a piping bag fitted with a small plain tip and fill the indentation on each cookie with chocolate to form the spider's body. Then pipe eight legs coming out of the spider body. Chill in the refrigerator for 30 minutes, or until the chocolate sets.

make it ahead Store the cookies in an airtight container in the refrigerator for up to 5 days.

tidbits The cookies can also be used for your Christmas celebrations as Sunbutter Blossoms. Instead of piping the spiders on the cookies, allow the chocolate to cool enough to hold its shape, then pipe chocolate kisses onto the cooled cookies.

Clockwise from top: sunbutter chocolate cups, caramel-filled chocolate candies, dirt cups, and spider cookies

dirt cups

Creepy, crawly jelly worms burrow within a layer of rich chocolate pudding with a crumble of dirtlike chocolate cake on top (pictured on page 207)! There are three different layers to this confection, so see my notes below on how to divide the steps and make it ahead. The gummy worm recipe makes more than you will need for the cups, so serve them in a bowl on their own as a nice candy alternative for the kids.

MAKES 8 CUPS

pudding

2¼ cups full-fat coconut milk

2½ teaspoons unflavored gelatin powder

½ cup pure maple syrup

¼ cup natural cocoa powder

1 teaspoon pure vanilla extract

Pinch of fine sea salt

gummy worms

2 cups water

3 tablespoons unflavored gelatin powder

½ cup light-colored raw honey

½ cup cherry juice concentrate

1 tablespoon freshly squeezed lemon juice

dirt

3 unfilled Whoopie Pie cookies (page 61), crumbled

To make the pudding, pour ¼ cup of the coconut milk into a heatproof bowl. Sprinkle the gelatin over the top and set aside to bloom for 5 minutes.

Heat the remaining 2 cups of coconut milk, the maple syrup, cocoa powder, vanilla extract, and salt in a saucepan over medium-high heat for 5 minutes. Whisk the hot mixture into the gelatin and continue whisking until all of the gelatin dissolves. Press a piece of plastic wrap directly on top of the pudding and chill in the refrigerator for 6 hours, or until completely set. Using an electric handheld mixer or a whisk, beat the chilled pudding on high speed until creamy.

To make the gummy worms, pour ½ cup of the water into a large bowl and sprinkle the gelatin over the top. Set aside to bloom for 5 minutes. Bring the remaining 1½ cups water and the honey to a boil in a saucepan, then pour it into the bloomed gelatin and whisk until the gelatin fully dissolves. Stir in the cherry juice concentrate and lemon juice.

Gather 50 flexible plastic drinking straws together with a rubber band and place them in a cup that is 2 to 3 inches wide and 5 to 6 inches tall. Trim the ends of the straws so they are slightly shorter than the cup. Pour the liquid into the straws until the liquid has fully submerged the straws in the cup. Refrigerate for 6 hours, or until set. Pull the straws out of the glass and place them on a cutting board. Using a rolling pin, start at one end and roll the worms one at a time out of the straws.

Spoon the pudding into eight 8-ounce see-through glass or plastic cups and place a few of the gummy worms on top of each cup. Sprinkle with the dirt (cookie crumbs) and serve.

make it ahead The pudding, gummy worms, and cookies will keep in the refrigerator for up to 1 week. Store them separately and assemble the night before serving. Cover and refrigerate until ready to serve.

sunbutter chocolate cups

Reduce the guilt this Halloween by trading these chocolates for the candies laden with high-fructose corn syrup and artificial coloring that your kids bring home after trick-or-treating. Use the chocolate shells for homemade sunbutter cups (pictured on page 207), caramel-filled treats, or any filling your little ghouls desire. A candy thermometer is used here, so be sure to have one on hand.

MAKES 12 CANDIES

sunbutter filling

½ cup unsweetened sunflower seed butter

⅓ cup pure maple syrup

¼ cup arrowroot powder

2 tablespoons melted raw cacao butter

1 teaspoon palm shortening, softened

¼ teaspoon pure vanilla extract

¼ teaspoon fine sea salt

chocolate shells

3 ounces raw cacao butter, chopped

2½ tablespoons pure maple syrup

⅓ cup plus 1 tablespoon natural cocoa powder

Pinch of fine sea salt

¼ teaspoon pure vanilla extract

Line one 12-cavity muffin pan with paper cupcake liners.

To make the sunbutter filling, combine the sunflower seed butter, maple syrup, arrowroot, cacao butter, palm shortening, vanilla, and salt in a bowl and mix until fully combined. Place it in the freezer to thicken for 15 minutes.

To make the chocolate shells, bring 2 inches of water in a saucepan to a simmer. Put the cacao butter in a glass bowl and set it over the simmering water, creating a double boiler. Whisk constantly for about 15 minutes, until the cacao butter is fully melted and reaches 100°F to 105°F on a thermometer. Turn off the heat and move the glass bowl to a cooler surface. Adding one ingredient at a time, gently whisk in the maple syrup, cocoa powder, salt, and vanilla just until combined. Once you've added all of the ingredients, switch to a rubber spatula and gently stir until cooled. The chocolate should be smooth and shiny, with a slightly thickened liquid consistency. Put 1 teaspoon of the chocolate into each cupcake liner and use a small, clean paintbrush or the back of the spoon to spread the chocolate in a very thin layer on the bottom and draw it ¼ inch up the sides. Set the remaining chocolate aside for later use. Put the muffin pan in the freezer for 10 minutes, or until the chocolate hardens.

Take the hardened chocolate shells out of the freezer. Scoop up 1 tablespoon of the filling and roll it into a ball between your palms. Flatten it into a ¼-inch-thick disk and place it in a chocolate shell, leaving a very thin border open between the filling and sides of the chocolate shell . Leave room at the top for a thin layer of chocolate, which you will add after the filling sets. Repeat to fill the remaining shells. Return the shells to the freezer for 10 minutes for the filling to set.

Remove from the freezer and use a spoon to spread a thin layer of chocolate over the sunbutter filling. Freeze for 10 additional minutes to harden. Remove the cups from the pan; peel away the liners, and serve or store the cups (see below).

VARIATION

Caramel-Filled Chocolate Candies For this variation, use a silicone candy mold with thirty 1-inch cavities and fill the chocolate shells with caramel (pictured on page 207). Make the chocolate shell recipe as above but pour ½ teaspoon chocolate into each cavity, filling it one-fourth full, and freeze until hardened, about 10 minutes.

To make the caramel filling, in a heavy saucepan, combine ½ cup light-colored raw honey, ¼ cup coconut sugar, 6 tablespoons full-fat coconut milk, 1½ teaspoons palm shortening or ghee (page 325), and ¼ teaspoon fine sea salt. Bring to a simmer over medium heat. Cook, swirling the saucepan occasionally to keep the mixture from burning, until a candy thermometer reads 240°F, about 15 minutes. Remove from the heat; whisk in ½ teaspoon pure vanilla extract. Let the caramel cool for 10 minutes, until it reaches 190°F. Turn it out onto a piece of parchment paper to cool, spreading it into a thin layer.

When the caramel is cool to the touch, roll it into small blueberry-size balls and place them on top of the layer of hardened chocolate. Press down to flatten the tops and leave a small border between the caramel and sides of the mold. Return to the freezer for 10 minutes to set.

Remove from the freezer and cover the caramel with the remaining chocolate. Freeze for another 10 minutes to harden. Remove the candies from the mold and serve or store as for the cups.

make it ahead Store in an airtight container in the refrigerator for up to 1 month or in the freezer for up to 6 months. Defrost the candies overnight in the refrigerator, then let them sit at room temperature for 10 minutes before serving.

tidbits If the chocolate mixture solidifies before the last step, place the bowl in a larger bowl filled with hot water. Gently stir the chocolate until it has reached the desired consistency, then remove it from the water bath.

If the caramel is too thin after cooling, place the pan back on the stove and simmer over medium heat for 5 minutes longer.

caramel apples

I remember passing by a chocolate factory in Colorado when I was a kid and always eyeing the old-fashioned, gooey, caramel-dipped apples. We'd get one caramel apple a year, and I would make it last in the refrigerator for a couple of days, just slicing off bits at a time. This dairy-free version uses coconut milk, unrefined honey, and low-glycemic coconut sugar in place of the typical milk, corn syrup, and white sugar. The temperature of the caramel is important in ensuring it sticks to the apple, so be sure to have a candy thermometer on hand for this recipe.

MAKES 8 APPLES

8 crisp apples, such as Fuji

1 cup light-colored raw honey

½ cup coconut sugar

¾ cup full-fat coconut milk

1 tablespoon palm shortening or ghee (page 325)

½ teaspoon fine sea salt

1 teaspoon pure vanilla extract

Chopped almonds, shredded unsweetened dried coconut, or mini chocolate chips, for coating

Wash and dry the fruit well to remove any waxy coating (see Tidbits below). Insert a wooden craft stick or small branch into each apple and set the apples on a tray lined with parchment paper. Refrigerate the tray to chill for 1 hour.

In a heavy saucepan, combine the honey, coconut sugar, coconut milk, palm shortening, and salt. Bring to a simmer over medium heat. Turn down the heat to low and continue to simmer, swirling the pan occasionally to keep it from burning, until a candy thermometer reads 235°F, about 12 minutes. Remove from the heat and whisk in the vanilla. Let the caramel cool until it reaches 190°F, 10 to 15 minutes.

One at a time, hold a chilled apple by the stick, dip it into the warm caramel mixture, and turn to coat. While the caramel is still warm, sprinkle with chopped nuts, shredded coconut, or mini chocolate chips. Place the coated apples on a piece of parchment paper to set. Work quickly because the caramel sets up fast.

make it ahead Wrap the cooled apples in plastic wrap and store them in the refrigerator for up to 3 days. Bring to room temperature to soften the caramel before serving.

tidbits Apples from the store often have a wax coating on them, which needs to be removed before you can coat them in caramel. Mix together a solution of hot water, a splash of lemon juice, and a pinch of baking soda and soak the apples in it for a few minutes, then remove and thoroughly dry.

If the caramel is too thin after cooling, place the pan back on the stove and simmer over medium heat for 5 minutes longer.

mummy dogs

The dough on these edible mummies becomes golden and crisp and will remind you of pigs in a blanket. Cutting a pattern on the dough before baking makes the finished dogs look like they're wrapped like mummies. The kids just love them!

MAKES 8 MUMMY DOGS

crust

1¼ cups blanched almond flour

½ cup arrowroot powder

1 egg, cold

1½ tablespoons cold water

¼ teaspoon fine sea salt

2 tablespoons palm shortening or ghee (page 325)

8 nitrate-free, grass-fed all-beef hot dogs

1 egg

1 tablespoon water

Mustard or ketchup (page 328), for serving

To make the crust, combine the almond flour, arrowroot, egg, water, and salt in a food processor. Process for 10 seconds, or until mixed. Add the palm shortening, spacing out where the tablespoons are dropped into the dough. Pulse 4 or 5 times, until dough has the texture of pea-size bits. Gather the dough into a tight ball and flatten it into a disk. Wrap tightly and refrigerate for 24 hours.

Preheat the oven to 375°F. Lightly grease a baking sheet.

Roll the dough out between two sheets of parchment paper into an oval ⅛ inch thick. Cut the oval into eight 2½ by 6½-inch rectangles.

Dry the hot dogs well with a towel. Wrap a dough rectangle around each hot dog and seal at one end, leaving ½ inch uncovered. Use a knife to cut shallow slits in the dough to create the look of cloth mummy straps. Arrange on the prepared baking sheet.

Whisk together the egg and water and brush it over the dough. Bake for 20 minutes, or until the dough is golden.

If desired, using a toothpick, dot mustard on the hot dogs for eyes. Serve hot, with the condiments for dipping.

make it ahead The unbaked dough-wrapped hot dogs can be stored on the baking sheet, tightly wrapped, in the refrigerator for up to 3 days. Bring to room temperature and brush with the egg wash prior to baking.

witches' fingers

These knobby garlic bread-stick fingers may just put a spell on you!
Dip them in your favorite marinara sauce for a spooky snack.

MAKES 12 BREAD STICKS

2 tablespoons ghee
(page 325)

2 cloves garlic, crushed

1¼ cups blanched
almond flour

1 egg

2 teaspoons extra-virgin
olive oil

1 teaspoon light-colored
raw honey

1 teaspoon chopped fresh
rosemary

¼ teaspoon fine sea salt

¼ teaspoon garlic salt

¼ teaspoon baking soda

12 whole raw almonds

Marinara sauce, for serving

Preheat the oven to 350°F. Line a baking sheet with parchment paper.

Heat the ghee and garlic in a small skillet over low heat and keep on low
while you make the bread sticks.

Combine the almond flour, egg, olive oil, honey, rosemary, salt, garlic
salt, and baking soda in the bowl of a stand mixer fitted with the beater
attachment, or use an electric handheld beater. Mix on medium speed
until a ball of dough forms. Divide the dough into 12 equal portions
and roll each into a ball. Using your fingertips, roll each piece of dough
out into a finger shape, about 4 inches long. If the dough begins to crack,
wet your fingertips slightly and continue rolling. Use your fingers to
create knotted knuckles and a knife to make light creases in the dough.
Press the almonds halfway down at the ends of the bread sticks to create
fingernails. Place the bread sticks on the prepared baking sheet, spacing
them evenly apart. Brush with the garlic-infused ghee.

Bake for 12 minutes, turning over halfway through. Cool on a wire rack
for 15 minutes, and serve warm with hot marinara sauce for dipping.

make it ahead Form the fingers, place them on the prepared baking sheet,
and wrap tightly. Store in the refrigerator for up to 2 days and bring to room
temperature before baking.

tidbits Look for a jar of marinara sauce that is free of sugar and soybean oil,
or make the homemade version from my first cookbook, *Against All Grain*.

autumn dinner party

Curry Pumpkin Soup

*Roasted Autumn
Harvest Salad*

Butternut Sage Carbonara

♦♦♦

Chai-Poached Pears

♦♦♦

Spiced Apple Hot Toddy

While the kids sort through their trick-or-treating bounty, serve the adults a beautiful and sophisticated autumnal meal. Start with a roasted harvest fruit salad and curried pumpkin soup, and follow with butternut sage pasta and a creamy, dairy-free carbonara sauce.

When my siblings and I were growing up, my dad always stole a few pieces of our candy after dinner to pay the "Dad Tax." But a spiked apple cider hot toddy and poached pears makes for a healthier and more refined dessert.

This menu would also be lovely to serve at a dinner party any time during the fall season. I love to put on some music from Vince Guaraldi, light a fire in the fireplace, and enjoy this cozy autumn meal with family and friends.

As we say in my family, Happy Fallidays!

curry pumpkin soup

My grandmother would prepare a big batch of pumpkin soup for the adults to eat while the kids went out to get their treats for the night, and my mom took on this tradition when we were growing up. This is my rendition of the recipe she has been using for decades.

SERVES 6

2 sugar or pie pumpkins (about 2 pounds each)

2 teaspoons fine sea salt

½ teaspoon freshly ground white pepper

2½ tablespoons extra-virgin olive oil

4 carrots, peeled and quartered

1 yellow onion, quartered

5 cloves garlic, peeled

6 cups chicken stock (page 327)

1½ teaspoons ground cinnamon

1 teaspoon ground ginger

½ teaspoon ground cumin

½ teaspoon ground coriander

½ teaspoon ground allspice

2 bay leaves

2 tablespoons pure maple syrup

1 cup almond milk (page 320)

½ cup full-fat coconut milk

6 ounces sweet Italian sausage, casings removed and meat crumbled

⅓ cup fresh sage leaves

tidbits You can substitute 6 (15-ounce) cans of organic pure pumpkin puree for the roasted pumpkins.

Preheat the oven to 400°F. Line a baking sheet with parchment paper.

Cut the pumpkins in half and remove the seeds and stringy pulp. Sprinkle the flesh side of the pumpkin halves with ½ teaspoon of the salt and ¼ teaspoon of the white pepper, then place the pumpkin halves, cut side down, on the prepared baking sheet. Drizzle the pumpkins with 1 tablespoon of the olive oil. Scatter the carrots, onion, and garlic around the pumpkins on the baking sheet. Roast for 45 minutes, or until the pumpkin is soft.

Scoop out the pumpkin flesh and discard the skins. Combine the pumpkin flesh, roasted vegetables, and 2 cups of stock in a blender and puree until smooth.

Heat the remaining 1½ tablespoons olive oil in a stockpot over medium-high heat. Add the cinnamon, ginger, cumin, coriander, allspice, and bay leaves. Stir constantly for 30 seconds, then add the remaining 4 cups stock, the maple syrup, and the pureed mixture. Bring to a boil, then lower the heat and simmer for 15 minutes. Remove the bay leaves. Season to taste with the remaining 1½ teaspoons salt and ¼ teaspoon white pepper. Stir in the almond and coconut milks, then turn the heat to low and keep the soup warm.

Put the sausage in a skillet over medium heat and cook for 5 to 7 minutes, until browned. Add the sage leaves and continue sautéing until the sage leaves are crispy and the sausage is cooked through. Drain and serve on top of the soup as a garnish.

make it ahead Make the soup up to 3 days in advance and reheat over medium-low heat. To freeze, refrigerate the soup until it is cool, then freeze in an airtight container for up to 3 months. Thaw in the refrigerator overnight, then reheat in a saucepan over medium-low heat. Cook the sausage and sage just before serving.

roasted autumn harvest salad

Roasting the fruits for this salad in a little balsamic vinegar and olive oil provides a beautiful depth of flavor and a natural sweetness that balances the acidity of the dressing. Once assembled, this is a stunning salad, and the toasted hazelnuts add a lovely crunch.

SERVES 6

6 figs, quartered

1 cup red seedless grapes

1 tart apple, cored and cut into thin wedges

½ cup hazelnuts

1 tablespoon balsamic vinegar

2 teaspoons extra-virgin olive oil

1 head radicchio, torn into bite-size pieces

6 cups baby romaine

2 cups baby arugula

dressing

¼ cup extra-virgin olive oil

2 tablespoons apple cider vinegar

1 tablespoon minced shallot

2 teaspoons whole-grain mustard

1 teaspoon chopped fresh thyme

Fine sea salt and freshly ground black pepper

Preheat the oven to 400°F.

Toss the figs, grapes, apple, hazelnuts, vinegar, and olive oil together and spread the fruits and nuts out evenly on a rimmed baking sheet. Roast for 15 minutes, gently tossing once halfway through, until the fruit has softened. Remove from the oven and cool for 15 minutes.

To make the dressing, whisk together the olive oil, vinegar, shallot, mustard, thyme, and salt and pepper.

Toss the radicchio, romaine, and arugula with the dressing. Divide the greens among plates, top each with some of the roasted fruits, and serve.

make it ahead One day before serving, in a bowl, toss the fruit in the vinegar and oil, wrap the bowl tightly in plastic wrap, and refrigerate. Wash and dry the lettuces up to 3 days in advance and store wrapped in damp paper towels in resealable bags in the refrigerator. Make the dressing up to 1 week in advance and store in an airtight container in the refrigerator.

tidbits Use rehydrated figs or substitute pears if you are unable to locate fresh figs. If cheese is tolerated, crumble a little chèvre or blue cheese on top.

butternut sage carbonara

Butternut squash is processed through a spiralizer to create this grain-free pasta dish. Topped with a creamy and rich garlic sauce and crunchy pancetta and sage leaves, it makes a beautiful dish to serve your guests on a cold, autumn night.

SERVES 6

8 ounces pancetta, diced

¼ cup fresh sage leaves, coarsely chopped

1 cup diced yellow onion

4 cloves garlic, minced

1 cup cashew milk (page 324) or any store-bought unsweetened cashew milk

1½ teaspoons freshly squeezed lemon juice

1 teaspoon fine sea salt

¼ teaspoon freshly ground black pepper, plus more for serving

2 egg yolks

3 pounds butternut squash

2 tablespoons ghee (page 325) or coconut oil

¼ cup walnuts, toasted and coarsely chopped

tidbits The bulbous part of the butternut squash holds the seeds and stringy flesh, which is why it is not used for making noodles. Dice it up and add it to a breakfast hash, or, if you have small children or babies in the house, make it into a puree.

Heat a stockpot over medium heat. Add the pancetta and cook for 8 minutes, then add the sage leaves and continue cooking for 2 to 3 minutes, until the pancetta and sage are crisp. Use a slotted spoon to transfer to a plate, leaving the grease in the pot.

Return the pot to the stove over medium heat, add the onion and garlic, and sauté for 3 to 5 minutes, until the garlic is toasted and the onion is translucent. Add the cashew milk and bring to a boil. Reduce the heat to medium-low and simmer for 10 minutes, or until the onion is soft. Transfer the mixture to a blender and add the lemon juice, salt, and pepper. Blend on high for 30 seconds. Add the egg yolks and blend again for 15 seconds.

Remove the bulbous part of the squash and save it for another use. Peel the long, slender neck of the squash until the orange flesh is visible. Cut the squash in half lengthwise so you have two pieces about 3 inches long. Use a spiralizer and the wider noodle blade, or a julienne slicer, to create noodles.

Wipe out the pot and return it to the stove over medium heat. Add the ghee and butternut noodles and sauté for 5 to 7 minutes, or until the noodles are crisp-tender.

Divide the noodles among serving bowls and top with a drizzle of sauce, the crisp pancetta, sage, walnuts, and some pepper.

make it ahead Cook the pancetta and sage leaves up to 2 days in advance and store in an airtight container in the refrigerator. Make the sauce up to 2 days in advance and store in an airtight container in the refrigerator. Cut the squash into noodles and store them submerged in a bowl of water and tightly covered for up to 1 day. Cook as directed and bring the sauce to room temperature before adding it to the hot noodles. Reheat the pancetta and sage on the stove.

chai-poached pears

This dessert is simple to prepare but makes an elegant ending to an autumn meal. The pears are poached in a sweet and boldly spiced black tea and served warm with my favorite of all dessert toppings, whipped cream.

SERVES 6

8 cups water

8 black tea bags

½ cup pure maple syrup

¼ cup coconut sugar

1 cinnamon stick

1 tablespoon pumpkin pie spice

2 whole star anise

1 teaspoon pure vanilla extract

6 ripe but firm Bosc pears

Whipped cream (page 332)

2 tablespoons raw pistachios, lightly toasted and chopped

Combine the water, tea bags, maple syrup, coconut sugar, cinnamon stick, pumpkin pie spice, star anise, and vanilla extract in a large saucepan. Bring to a boil, then cover and reduce the heat to a simmer. Steep over low heat for 30 minutes. Strain the mixture through a fine-mesh sieve, then return the liquid to the pan.

Peel the pears and core them from the bottom, leaving the top stem intact. Place them in the pot and bring the tea back to a low boil. Poach the pears over medium-low heat for 30 to 40 minutes, until tender. Using a slotted spoon, remove the pears from the cooking liquid and place them in serving bowls. Increase the heat to high and bring the liquid to a boil. Boil for 15 minutes, or until the liquid has reduced to a syrup.

Spoon the syrup over the pears and into the bottom of the bowls. Serve with a dollop of whipped cream and a sprinkle of toasted pistachios.

make it ahead The pears can be poached and the poaching liquid reduced up to 2 days in advance. Store the pears in the liquid in an airtight container in the refrigerator. Reheat the pears in a saucepan with the syrup over low heat.

spiced apple hot toddy

Warm up on a cold autumn night with this spiced apple and bourbon drink. Whiskey and bourbon are not certified gluten-free, although many people feel that the distillation process removes the gluten from the liquor, making it safe to consume. That said, drink responsibly and do not risk it if you have celiac disease. See the Tidbits for substitution ideas.

SERVES 6

2¼ cups apple cider or unfiltered apple juice

3 tablespoons light-colored raw honey

4 cinnamon sticks, plus more for garnish

2 teaspoons whole cloves

1 cup plus 2 tablespoons bourbon

3 tablespoons freshly squeezed lemon juice

Apple slices, for garnish

In a small saucepan, combine the apple cider, honey, cinnamon sticks, and cloves. Bring to a boil, then remove from the heat and steep, covered, for 15 minutes. Strain out the solids, then stir in the bourbon and lemon juice. Divide among 6 mugs and garnish each mug with an apple slice and a cinnamon stick.

make it ahead The juice and spices can be steeped and strained up to 3 days in advance. Store in the refrigerator and gently reheat before mixing in the bourbon and lemon juice.

tidbits Substitute gluten-free brandy or tequila for the bourbon, or, for a nonalcoholic beverage, use black tea.

thanksgiving

I adore this holiday because it is a time when my family and friends, from near and far, come together and create memories year after year. We play board games, watch parades, have a lovely meal, and end the day with a friendly game of flag football. With such a busy life, I appreciate the opportunity to take a moment during the month of November to remember how blessed I am. After the trials and tragedies of the last few years, my family is especially thankful for our health: both for my recovery from illness and the fact that we have the honor of raising two beautiful, healthy boys.

I was a simple eater (a nice way to say picky) growing up, and I only ate turkey, mashed potatoes, gravy, and a little helping of green beans. No sweet potatoes, bread, cranberry sauce, or even stuffing! I did not like my foods touching on the plate, so I wasn't even able to experience the glee that comes from flavors mixing together or getting a little cranberry on top of a bite of mashed potatoes with a little turkey and a splash of gravy. My, how I was missing out.

The recipes in this chapter make it possible for everyone to enjoy the holiday and its traditional food whether you and your guests are grain-free or conventional eaters. All of the old-time favorites like stuffing, green bean casserole, and cranberry sauce are here, and I've even come up with a new way to enjoy sweet potatoes that I think is so good you may add it to your weekly meal plan year-round. And since it wouldn't be Thanksgiving in my house without a pie for dessert, I've included three pie recipes, including a pecan pie that will more than stand up to its corn syrup– and gluten-filled counterpart. Or just finish the night with a creamy and comforting spice-laced latte.

It's true that a lot of work goes into hosting a Thanksgiving feast, but thankfully the meal usually involves community. (And leftovers! Check out CelebrationsCookbook.com/thanksgiving-leftovers for recipes.) Share this book with your friends and family and have no shame in assigning some of the dishes to them to free up your time (and oven space). I am sure that with this meal, you will all be able to sit around the table afterward ruminating on the fabulous, nourishing food you enjoyed together and the many things in your life to give thanks for.

Happy Thanksgiving!

menu

❖❖❖

Herbed Drop Biscuits

Roasted Garlic Mashed Cauliflower

Cranberry Sauce

Green Bean Casserole with Crispy Shallots

Smoky Candied Bacon Sweet Potatoes

Roasted Brussels Sprouts with Bacon Jam

Apple Sausage Stuffing

Brined and Roasted Turkey

❖❖❖

Maple Pumpkin Pie

Apple Pie

Chocolate Pecan Tart

❖❖❖

Pumpkin Spice Latte

herbed drop biscuits

The combination of cashew, almond, and coconut flour gives these biscuits a one-of-a-kind flavor and crusty exterior. And the moist crumbly center is fragrant from the fresh herbs added to the dough.

MAKES 12 BISCUITS

1½ cups (about 220g) whole raw cashews

3 eggs, separated

¾ teaspoon apple cider vinegar

¼ cup almond milk (page 320) or store-bought unsweetened almond milk

⅓ cup coconut flour

¼ cup blanched almond flour

3 fresh sage leaves, torn

1 sprig rosemary, needles stripped from stem

¾ teaspoon fine sea salt

1 teaspoon baking soda

¼ cup palm shortening, ghee (page 325), or grass-fed unsalted butter, softened

Preheat the oven to 325°F. Line a baking sheet with parchment paper.

Process the cashews in a food processor for 10 seconds, or until ground to a fine flour. Add the egg yolks, vinegar, and almond milk, then process again for 10 seconds, or until the mixture resembles a thick paste. Add the coconut flour, almond flour, herbs, salt, and baking soda and process again.

Either by hand with a whisk or with an electric handheld mixer, beat the egg whites in a separate bowl until soft peaks form. Add the egg whites and palm shortening to the food processor, then pulse 6 to 8 times, until the egg whites are just incorporated.

Using two spoons or a large cookie scoop, drop lumps of dough onto the prepared baking sheet, spacing them 1 inch apart.

Bake for 30 minutes, or until golden brown. Cool on a wire rack and serve warm.

make it ahead Bake these biscuits, then cool, pack them in an airtight container separated from one another with parchment paper, and freeze for up to 6 months. Defrost overnight in the refrigerator and place in a warm oven to reheat before serving.

tidbits Substitute any herb of your choice for the herbs listed here. For an even richer biscuit, brush the tops with a little melted ghee and sprinkle with garlic powder before baking.

roasted garlic mashed cauliflower

Mashed cauliflower is such a great, low-carb stand-in for mashed potatoes. I roast garlic and puree it with the cauliflower to give it a smooth but robust flavor.

SERVES 10 TO 12

8 cloves garlic, unpeeled

2 tablespoons extra-virgin olive oil

2 heads cauliflower, trimmed into florets

⅓ cup chicken stock (page 327)

5 tablespoons melted ghee (page 325)

2 teaspoons fine sea salt

¼ teaspoon freshly ground black pepper, plus more for garnish

Chopped fresh thyme, for garnish

Preheat the oven to 425°F.

Put the garlic in a small, heatproof dish and drizzle with the olive oil. Cover and roast for 15 minutes. Set aside to cool.

While the garlic is roasting, put the cauliflower in a saucepan with ½ inch of water. Cover and steam over medium-high heat for 10 minutes, or until tender. Drain well and transfer the cauliflower to a food processor.

Squeeze the papery garlic skins to release the cloves. Add the garlic to the food processor along with the stock, ghee, salt, and pepper. Process until smooth and fluffy. Transfer to a serving bowl, garnish with the pepper and thyme, and serve warm.

make it ahead Make this dish up to 4 days in advance. Reheat in a dry skillet over medium-low heat until warmed through, about 10 minutes, or in a covered dish in a 350°F oven.

tidbits If cauliflower isn't for you, triple the recipe for the parsnip-turnip puree that accompanies the short ribs on page 79, and serve it instead.

cranberry sauce

I grew up on the canned version of this holiday favorite. I actually never liked it and skipped over the jellylike substance at every Thanksgiving. Now that I've made it at home and know that what I am eating is not full of refined sugar, I've grown to love the tart flavor with my turkey and stuffing.

MAKES 4 CUPS

1 tablespoon unflavored gelatin powder

½ cup water

2 (12-ounce) packages fresh cranberries

1 cup freshly squeezed orange juice

1 cup light-colored raw honey

2 teaspoons finely grated orange zest

½ teaspoon ground nutmeg

½ teaspoon ground cinnamon

In a small bowl, sprinkle the gelatin over the water and set aside to bloom.

Mix the cranberries, orange juice, honey, orange zest, nutmeg, and cinnamon in a saucepan over medium-high heat. Bring the sauce to a boil, then reduce the heat to medium and simmer until the berries begin to break open, about 20 minutes. Pour in the bloomed gelatin and whisk until dissolved.

Remove from the heat and transfer to a bowl. Cool to room temperature, then cover and refrigerate for 4 hours, or until thickened. Serve chilled.

make it ahead The sauce can be stored in an airtight container in the refrigerator for up to 1 week or in the freezer for up to 6 months. Defrost overnight in the refrigerator before serving.

green bean casserole with crispy shallots

SERVES 10 TO 12

1 cup (about 150g) whole raw cashews

2 tablespoons ghee (page 325) or extra-virgin olive oil

8 ounces cremini mushrooms, halved

1 shallot, peeled and chopped

1 clove garlic, crushed

2 tablespoons sherry (optional)

1 cup water

1¾ cups chicken stock, (page 327)

1½ teaspoons fine sea salt

½ teaspoon freshly ground black pepper

1 teaspoon fresh thyme leaves

2 pounds haricots verts (thin green beans), ends trimmed

topping

½ cup palm shortening, bacon fat, or ghee (page 325), for frying

2 shallots, peeled and thinly sliced into rings

tidbits To use green beans instead of haricots verts, blanch the beans in a pot of boiling water for 5 minutes, then transfer the beans using a slotted spoon to a bowl of ice cold water. Drain the beans, combine them with the sauce, and bake as directed.

Thanksgiving just doesn't feel the same without this creamy casserole, so I have re-created it *Against All Grain*–style, without the heavy cream, MSG, or gluten. I could eat the mushroom sauce in this dish by the spoonful.

Place the cashews in a bowl and cover them with boiling water. Soak for 1 hour.

Meanwhile, heat the ghee in a skillet over medium heat. Add the mushrooms, shallot, and garlic and sauté for 10 minutes, or until the mushrooms and shallot have softened. Pour in the sherry and simmer for 5 minutes to reduce the liquid.

Drain and rinse the cashews, transfer them to a blender, add the water, and blend until very smooth.

Add the mushroom mix, half of the stock, and the salt, pepper, and thyme to the blender and pulse a few times until the mushrooms are bite size. Pour the mixture into a bowl and stir in the remaining half of the stock. Set aside to cool for 15 minutes.

Preheat the oven to 350°F.

Combine the mushroom mixture with the haricots verts and spoon into a casserole dish. Bake, covered, for 30 minutes, until the beans are tender and the sauce is bubbling. Uncover and bake for 15 minutes more.

Meanwhile, to make the topping, heat the palm shortening in a small, deep saucepan over medium-high heat. Working in batches, panfry the shallots for about 5 minutes, until golden brown. Drain and cool in a single layer on a plate lined with paper towels.

Top the casserole with the crispy shallots and serve warm.

make it ahead Since this dish involves a few steps, it's helpful to do it in stages ahead of time. Make the sauce up to 3 days in advance and store in an airtight container in the refrigerator. Trim the haricots verts and store in a bowl of water, tightly covered, in the refrigerator for up to 5 days. Prepare the assembled casserole up to 2 days in advance, cover, and store in the refrigerator. Bring to room temperature, then bake as directed.

smoky candied bacon sweet potatoes

The flavors of fall come together in this dish of spiced roasted sweet potatoes with candied pecans and bacon. I was never a fan of sweet potatoes, or yams, growing up, so I skipped the classic candied yams with marshmallow and sugar topping. When I started eating Paleo and introduced them into my diet, I came up with ways to make them savory instead of sweet and enjoy them now. I often hear from anti-sweet potato folks that they love this dish!

SERVES 10 TO 12

3 pounds sweet potatoes, scrubbed but not peeled

6 ounces bacon, cut into 1-inch pieces

½ cup pecans, coarsely chopped

⅓ cup pure maple syrup

1 teaspoon chili powder

½ teaspoon fine sea salt

½ teaspoon ground cinnamon

¼ teaspoon cayenne pepper

Preheat the oven to 400°F. Line two rimmed baking sheets with parchment paper.

Cut the sweet potatoes into even 1-inch cubes. Toss them with the bacon, pecans, maple syrup, chili powder, salt, cinnamon, and cayenne in a bowl. Spread in a single layer on the prepared baking sheets.

Roast for 20 minutes. Stir and continue roasting for 15 minutes, or until tender. Turn the oven to broil and brown the potatoes for an additional 5 minutes. Watch the nuts closely and pull the baking sheets out early if they begin to burn. Serve hot.

make it ahead Combine all of the ingredients and store in an airtight container in the refrigerator for up to 3 days before cooking. Bring to room temperature, then bake as directed.

tidbits There's always a lot of confusion surrounding yams and sweet potatoes. Either will work here, but I go for the orange-fleshed yam for this recipe to add some color to the dinner buffet.

roasted brussels sprouts with bacon jam

Growing up, I used to shiver at the words "Brussels sprouts." That is because I'd only had them boiled with onions, and I couldn't stand them. Now, I absolutely love Brussels sprouts, especially when they have this tangy and smoky bacon jam spooned over the top.

bacon jam

1½ pounds thick-cut bacon

1 cup diced shallots

1 yellow onion, diced

4 cloves garlic, chopped

1 tablespoon natural cocoa powder

1 teaspoon chili powder

1 teaspoon sweet paprika

½ teaspoon ground ginger

½ teaspoon ground cinnamon

½ cup water

½ cup apple cider

¼ cup coconut sugar

¼ cup pure maple syrup

4 pounds Brussels sprouts, trimmed and then halved if large

1½ teaspoons fine sea salt

¾ teaspoon freshly ground black pepper

To make the bacon jam, cook the bacon in a large cast-iron skillet over medium heat until crisp. Remove the bacon from the pan and reserve the bacon grease. Set the bacon aside to cool, then coarsely chop.

Heat 2 tablespoons of the bacon grease in the same skillet over medium heat. Add the shallots, onion, and garlic and cook for 5 to 7 minutes, until the onion is translucent. Stir in the cocoa powder, chili powder, paprika, ginger, and cinnamon. Stir and cook for 1 minute, or until fragrant. Stir in the water, apple cider, coconut sugar, and maple syrup, stirring up any browned bits from the pan bottom. Add the bacon and bring to a boil, then lower the heat to a simmer. Simmer, uncovered, for 45 minutes, stirring occasionally, until the liquid has mostly evaporated and the onion is very soft. Carefully transfer the contents of the skillet to a food processor, or use a handheld immersion blender, and pulse once or twice to coarsely chop. Set aside at room temperature until you are ready to serve.

Preheat the oven to 400°F.

Toss the Brussels sprouts in ¼ cup of the bacon grease and season with the salt and pepper. Spread the Brussels sprouts out in a single layer on two large rimmed baking sheets. Roast for 25 minutes, then increase the temperature to 425°F. Toss the sprouts, then roast for an additional 5 to 7 minutes, until crisp.

Toss the sprouts in ¼ cup of the bacon jam and serve, passing the rest of the jam on the side.

make it ahead Cool the bacon jam completely, then store in an airtight container in the refrigerator for up to 1 week or in the freezer for up to 6 months. Defrost in the refrigerator overnight, then reheat in a skillet over medium-low heat.

tidbits Save your eyes! Peel and quarter the shallots and onion, then throw them in a food processor and pulse until chopped.

apple sausage stuffing

Sweet sausage, crisp apple, and fresh herbs make this stuffing special.
I do not bake this stuffing in the bird for two reasons: the brined bird
will make it too salty and grain-free breads tend to get too soggy.
Bake two loaves of my blender bread or use your favorite store-bought
gluten-free bread in this recipe.

SERVES 10 TO 12

2 loaves blender bread
(page 323), cooled

7 tablespoons melted ghee
(page 325) or extra-virgin
olive oil

1 tablespoon extra-virgin
olive oil

2 ribs celery (leaves
included), chopped

1 yellow onion, chopped

2 cloves garlic, minced

8 ounces sweet Italian
sausage, casings removed
and meat crumbled

1 Fuji apple, cored and
chopped

½ cup cremini mushrooms,
chopped

3 sprigs parsley, chopped

1 sprig rosemary, needles
stripped from stem and
chopped

2 sprigs thyme, chopped

2 fresh sage leaves, chopped

¼ cup dry vermouth
(optional)

3 eggs, lightly beaten

2 teaspoons fine sea salt

½ teaspoon freshly ground
black pepper

1¼ cups turkey or chicken
stock (page 327)

Slice the loaves in half lengthwise to make four thin loaves total,
then cut them into 1-inch cubes.

Preheat the oven to 300°F. Toss the bread cubes with 5 tablespoons
of the melted ghee. Place on a baking sheet and toast in the oven for
30 minutes, turning occasionally, until the cubes are golden brown
and slightly dry.

Meanwhile, heat the olive oil in a large skillet over medium heat. Add
the celery, onion, garlic, sausage, apple, mushrooms, parsley, rosemary,
thyme, and sage and sauté for 15 minutes. Add the vermouth and bring
to a boil.

Preheat the oven to 350°F. Grease a 9 by 13-inch baking dish.

Toss the bread cubes with the sausage mixture, eggs, salt, pepper,
and turkey stock.

Transfer the stuffing to the prepared baking dish and drizzle the
remaining 2 tablespoons ghee on top. Cover and bake for 35 minutes.
Uncover and bake for 15 minutes, or until the top is golden. Serve hot.

make it ahead Prepare the loaves of bread up to 5 days in advance and
store, tightly wrapped, in the refrigerator. Sauté the sausage mixture up
to 2 days in advance and store in an airtight container in the refrigerator.
Assemble the stuffing just before baking.

brined and roasted turkey

SERVES 10 TO 12

brine

8 quarts water

1¼ cups coarse sea salt

4 bay leaves

1 (750-ml) bottle Pinot Grigio (or other dry white wine)

¼ cup light-colored raw honey or coconut sugar

8 cloves garlic, crushed

2 yellow onions, quartered

1 bunch fresh thyme

1 tablespoon allspice berries

1 tablespoon juniper berries

1 tablespoon peppercorns

2 teaspoons anise seeds

1 (12- to 16-pound) fresh or frozen and defrosted whole turkey, neck and giblets removed and saved for stock

A brine is a mixture of salt, liquid, and spices and is used to seal the outer pores of the turkey, trapping in all of the juices and tenderizing the meat. If your turkey is frozen, be sure to defrost it fully in the fridge before brining. You'll need to allow about 24 hours for each 5 pounds of frozen turkey you plan to thaw.

I think it is always best to go with a simple turkey preparation, especially after brining it. The mix of ghee and olive oil here helps create that crispy skin we all love, but you can also use duck or bacon fat if you want to stay away from dairy. I start the roasting at a high temperature to brown the skin and speed the process, then finish it at a lower temperature to ensure a moist turkey every time.

Turkey and mashed cauliflower are not the same to me without creamy seasoned gravy, but the way my dad and grandmother always made gravy was with cornstarch or wheat flour and artificial flavoring like Kitchen Bouquet. Here, I use the flavorful pan drippings with chicken stock and puree it with the roasted vegetables from the turkey pan to thicken it.

To make the brine, heat 1 quart of the water in a large stockpot over medium-high heat. Stir in the salt, bay leaves, wine, honey, garlic, onions, thyme, allspice, juniper, peppercorns, and anise seeds and continue stirring until the salt dissolves. Remove from the heat and pour in the remaining 7 quarts water. Let cool to room temperature. Pat the turkey dry and place it in a brining bag or a pot large enough to hold it submerged in the brine. Pour the brine over the bird so it is submerged and seal the bag or cover the pot. Place in the refrigerator for 24 hours.

CONTINUED

3 yellow onions, quartered

2 carrots, peeled and quartered

4 ribs celery, quartered

8 cloves garlic, 4 peeled and crushed and 4 whole with peels

1 whole lemon, halved

2 sprigs rosemary

1 bunch flat-leaf parsley

1 bunch thyme

¼ cup melted ghee (page 325)

¼ cup extra-virgin olive oil

pan gravy

Reserved onions, garlic, and celery from roasting pan

Pan drippings

1½ cups turkey or chicken stock (page 327), plus more as needed

Fine sea salt and freshly ground black pepper

Rinse the bird and pat dry, inside and out, with paper towels. Arrange it, breast side up, on a roasting rack set inside a roasting pan and allow it to stand at room temperature for 1 hour before roasting.

Remove all but one of the oven racks in the oven and position that rack in the bottom third of the oven. Preheat the oven to 500°F.

Place 1 onion, all of the carrots, half of the celery, and the peeled garlic cloves inside the cavity of the bird. Squeeze the juice of the lemon into the cavity and stuff the lemon halves inside with the rosemary, parsley, and thyme. Tie the drumsticks together with kitchen twine.

Combine the melted ghee and olive oil in a bowl and rub some of it all over the skin. Reserve the remainder for basting. Scatter the remaining 2 onions, 2 celery ribs, and whole garlic cloves on the bottom of the pan.

Roast the turkey for 30 minutes. Rotate the pan 180 degrees, baste the turkey with the remaining oil mixture, then reduce the oven temperature to 350°F. Continue roasting until a thermometer inserted into the thickest part of the thigh reads 165°F or the juices run clear when the thigh is pierced. A 12- to 14-pound bird will take 1½ to 2 hours longer (a 14- to 16-pound bird will take 2 to 2½ hours longer).

Let the turkey rest, loosely covered with aluminum foil, for 15 minutes before carving.

For the pan gravy, transfer the reserved onions and celery from the bottom of the roasting pan to a blender.

Pour the drippings from the pan into a fat separator and pour off the fat. Pour the drippings into the blender. Alternatively, tilt the pan and skim off as much fat as possible, then pour the drippings into the blender. Squeeze the roasted garlic out of the peels and add to the blender. Add the stock and puree on high speed until smooth and thick. Add more stock until it reaches a desired thickness. If the gravy is too thin, add a few pieces of onion from the cavity of the bird to thicken. Season with salt and pepper to taste. Note that the brine causes the gravy to be salty already, so you may not need to add any at all.

CONTINUED

brined and roasted turkey, continued

tidbits Don't have a pot large enough for brining the turkey? Try a cooler or a clean bucket that is big enough for the bird but small enough to fit in the fridge. Remove the shelves from the fridge, if necessary.

Do not bake your stuffing inside the cavity of a brined turkey and do not salt your gravy. There's enough salt already from the brine.

Roasting times may vary depending on the type of turkey you purchase. These times relate to an organic, pasture-raised bird, which tends to be slightly leaner than a conventional turkey.

Reheat leftover turkey in a covered dish with a small amount of turkey or chicken stock at the bottom to help keep it moist. Use other leftovers in the recipes that follow, or make a pot pie using extra pan gravy (see page 250) and my basic pie pastry (page 322).

Know your bird: While turkeys are in abundance at supermarkets during the holiday months, a good-quality turkey may need to be ordered in advance. Check with your local butcher, Whole Foods, or favorite vendor at your farmers' market toward the end of October to ensure you get it by the big day. I allot 1½ pounds of turkey per person when deciding how large of a bird to buy. This will give you enough for dinner and some left over for soups and sandwiches the next day. If possible, buy a 100 percent pasture-raised turkey, as it will be superior. The label ensures that the bird was allowed to roam freely and forage on the ground, as it was meant to. It also means the bird was not given a feed of soy, corn, or other grains. Heritage and organic birds are also great options.

maple pumpkin pie

This is my favorite dessert of the season, and I cannot wait for the excuse to make it every year. A little secret: my favorite way to eat it is cold, straight from the fridge, and sometimes for breakfast!

MAKES ONE 9-INCH PIE; SERVES 8 TO 10

pastry

Basic pie pastry (page 322), frozen for 1 hour

1 egg yolk

1 tablespoon full-fat coconut milk

filling

2 cups fresh pumpkin puree or 1 (15-ounce) can pure pumpkin

3 eggs

½ cup full-fat coconut milk

½ cup pure maple syrup or light-colored raw honey

1 teaspoon ground cinnamon

½ teaspoon ground ginger

½ teaspoon ground nutmeg

¼ teaspoon ground cloves

¼ teaspoon ground cardamom

½ teaspoon finely grated lemon zest

1 teaspoon pure vanilla extract

¼ teaspoon kosher salt

Whipped coconut cream (page 331) or whipped cream (page 332), for serving

Preheat the oven to 325°F and line a baking sheet with parchment paper.

Reserve one-fourth of the dough to make decorative toppings. Press the remaining dough into the bottom and up the sides of a 9-inch pie plate, using the palms of your hands to ensure the crust is even throughout. Press together any breaks in the dough, then crimp or flute the edges with your fingers. Cut a round of parchment paper to fit the bottom of the crust and fill with pie weights or dried beans. Freeze until firm, about 15 minutes.

Bake the pie shell for 10 minutes, remove the weights and parchment paper, and bake for 5 minutes more, or until the crust is golden. Cool completely on a wire rack.

Roll out the reserved pie pastry between two sheets of parchment paper. Use cookie cutters to cut out shapes. Make an egg wash by mixing together the egg yolk and coconut milk and brush onto the pastry shapes. Transfer to the prepared baking sheet and bake for 15 minutes, or until the shapes are golden. Cool completely on a wire rack.

Increase the oven temperature to 350°F. Place the pie shell on a rimmed baking sheet and brush the edges with the remaining egg wash.

To make the filling, whisk together the pumpkin, eggs, coconut milk, maple syrup, cinnamon, ginger, nutmeg, cloves, cardamom, lemon zest, vanilla, and salt. Pour the filling into the prepared pie shell. Bake for 15 minutes, then cover the crust with foil and continue baking for 20 minutes, or until the custard has set but still jiggles slightly in the center. Turn off the oven and leave it cracked open for 30 minutes while the pie cools.

Cool to room temperature on a wire rack, then place the decorative cutouts around the perimeter of the pie and place it in the refrigerator to fully set, about 2 hours. Serve with the whipped coconut cream.

make it ahead This pie keeps well, covered tightly with plastic wrap, for up to 3 days in the refrigerator and actually gets better with time.

apple pie

Here is an apple pie just like you remember it from Thanksgivings past, but without the grains and refined sugars. The combination of apple varieties creates a wonderful firm and soft texture with both sweet and tart notes.

MAKES ONE 9-INCH PIE;
SERVES 8 TO 10

Double recipe basic pie pastry (page 322), divided into 2 disks before freezing

4 Granny Smith apples, peeled, cored, and sliced

4 McIntosh apples, peeled, cored, and sliced

½ cup coconut sugar, plus 1 tablespoon for dusting

⅓ cup light-colored raw honey

2 tablespoons freshly squeezed lemon juice

2 teaspoons arrowroot powder

1 teaspoon ground cinnamon

½ teaspoon ground nutmeg

Pinch of freshly ground allspice

¼ teaspoon fine sea salt

1 egg yolk

1 tablespoon full-fat coconut milk

Whipped coconut cream (page 331) or whipped cream (page 332), for serving

Remove one pastry disk from the freezer and press it into the bottom and up the sides of a 9-inch pie plate, using the palms of your hands to ensure the crust is even throughout. Press together any breaks in the dough, then crimp or flute the edges with your fingers. Place in the refrigerator for 30 minutes.

Combine the apples, coconut sugar, honey, lemon juice, arrowroot powder, cinnamon, nutmeg, allspice, and salt in a bowl and toss to coat the apples well.

Preheat the oven to 350°F. Remove the second disk of pie pastry from the freezer and roll the dough out between two sheets of parchment paper into a circle about 11 inches in diameter and ¼ inch thick.

Pour the apples into the pastry-lined pie plate, heaping them in the center. Carefully flip the rolled dough on top of the apples and lightly tug on the parchment paper to release the dough on top of the pie. Seal the sides of the dough together by crimping with your fingers. The dough will likely crack or split; just gently work it back together with your fingers. Cut a few venting holes in the top crust.

To make an egg wash, whisk the egg yolk and coconut milk together and brush it all over the crust. Place the pie on a baking sheet and bake for 35 minutes. Cover the entire top of the pie with foil and continue baking for 30 minutes, or until the filling is bubbling and the crust is golden.

Remove the foil and cool the pie on a wire rack for 1 hour before serving. Serve warm with whipped coconut cream.

make it ahead Prepare the pie pastry and the apple filling up to 2 days in advance and store separately, tightly wrapped, in the refrigerator. Skip the freezer step for the crust, as it will firm up enough in the fridge. The baked pie keeps well, covered, at room temperature for 24 hours or refrigerated for up to 3 days.

chocolate pecan tart

With hints of maple and vanilla, this pecan pie is rich and gooey and rivals the processed version we all grew up eating. If you're not a chocolate lover, feel free to omit the dark chocolate from the filling.

SERVES 8 TO 10

Basic pie pastry (page 322), frozen for 1 hour

2 eggs

1 egg white

½ cup coconut sugar

¼ cup pure maple syrup

3 tablespoons melted ghee (page 325) or coconut oil

2 teaspoons pure vanilla extract

1½ cups pecan halves

½ cup chopped dark chocolate (85 percent cacao)

1 egg yolk

1 tablespoon full-fat coconut milk

Whipped coconut cream (page 331) or whipped cream (page 332), for serving

Preheat the oven to 350°F.

Press the pie pastry into the bottom and up the sides of an 11 by 7-inch tart pan with a removable base. Bake for 15 minutes, then cool on a wire rack.

Whisk together the whole eggs, egg white, coconut sugar, maple syrup, ghee, and vanilla. Chop ½ cup of the pecans and add them to the mixture with the dark chocolate. Pour the mixture into the prepared tart shell. Lightly arrange the remaining 1 cup pecans in a decorative pattern on top.

Make an egg wash by mixing the egg yolk with the coconut milk in a small bowl. Brush the exposed crust with the egg wash and bake for 15 minutes. Cover just the crust with foil or a pie shield and continue baking for 5 to 10 minutes, until the center is set.

Cool on a wire rack for several hours or overnight. Remove the pan sides and slice the tart into rectangles. Serve with the whipped coconut cream.

make it ahead This pie keeps well, covered, for up to 3 days at room temperature.

tidbits To bake this as a pie instead of a tart, press the dough into a 9-inch pie plate and double the filling recipe, then proceed as directed for the tart.

pumpkin spice latte

The PSL—it takes over every coffee shop in town as soon as September rolls around, but is full of sugar and artificial ingredients. Instead of spending your hard-earned money on a drink that doesn't even have pumpkin in the ingredients, make this one at home and enjoy it from the comfort of your living room.

SERVES 4

2 cups strongly brewed coffee or espresso

¾ cup almond milk (page 320)

¾ cup full-fat coconut milk

⅓ cup pure maple syrup

3 tablespoons pumpkin puree

1 teaspoon pumpkin pie spice

½ teaspoon pure vanilla extract

Combine all of the ingredients in a saucepan over medium-high heat. Simmer for 5 minutes, whisking occasionally, until heated through and slightly frothy on top.

Carefully transfer the liquid to a blender and cover the top with a towel. Blend on high for 30 seconds until foamy. Alternatively, use an immersion blender in the pot. Divide among 4 mugs and serve.

make it ahead To turn this into a coffee creamer, combine everything except the coffee. Stir the creamer into a hot cup of coffee or store it in an airtight container in the refrigerator for up to 1 week. To use the creamer in a single serving of latte, combine 1 part creamer to 2 parts coffee in a blender and blend until frothy. It also works well with chai tea.

tidbits If you open a can of pumpkin puree and don't use the whole thing, save the rest in an airtight container in the refrigerator for up to 3 days, or freeze it in ice cube trays, then store the frozen cubes in a resealable plastic bag in the freezer for up to 6 months. Use it in the various pumpkin recipes listed on my blog (againstallgrain.com).

christmas

christmas breakfast

We are a serious Christmas family. Our love for the holiday started with my grandmother on my mom's side, and the Christmas bug has been passed down through my mom to me and my siblings. We're chomping at the bit to play Christmas music, and we all enjoy gift giving; decorating our houses with nativities, twinkle lights, and trees; and watching every holiday special or sappy movie the television has to offer.

I will always remember the painstakingly long wait as a kid between waking up on Christmas morning and opening presents. My parents made my brother, sister, and me all sit down to a big breakfast beforehand, and the grown-ups always went back for seconds and then cleaned up the dishes to purposefully make us wait a little longer. (Or at least that's what we thought.)

Now that I have kids of my own—and Ryan and I usually spend Christmas Eve and Christmas morning packaging up last-minute gifts and readying the house—I like to prepare a breakfast the night before that can be thrown in the oven when we wake up. The egg casserole and cinnamon rolls fit the bill.

Merry Christmas morning!

menu

◆◆◆

Cinnamon Rolls

Sausage Breakfast Casserole

◆◆◆

Gingerbread Latte

cinnamon rolls

MAKES 10 ROLLS

dough

3 tablespoons white chia seeds

¾ cup hot water

1½ cups arrowroot powder

¾ cup raw cashew butter

¾ cup finely ground golden flaxseeds

½ cup coconut flour

¾ cup coconut sugar

2 tablespoons palm shortening, softened

1 tablespoon grain-free baking powder (page 325)

filling

⅓ cup ghee (page 325) or coconut oil, melted

¾ cup coconut sugar

⅓ cup light-colored raw honey

2 tablespoons ground cinnamon

1½ cups whipped cream (page 332), chilled for at least 6 hours

tidbits For a nut-free version, substitute raw tahini butter or sunflower seed butter for the cashew butter. For a nut-free glaze, use the glaze for the Lemon Lavender Bundt Cakes (page 197) but omit the lemon and lavender.

I created this roll especially for anyone who is egg-free (see Tidbits below for a nut-free substitution). If eggs and nuts are not a problem, use the dough recipe from the Caramel-Pecan Sticky Buns (page 88) with this filling and frosting.

Preheat the oven to 350°F. Line the bottom of a 10-inch pie plate or a quarter sheet pan with parchment paper. Lightly grease the sides of the dish.

To make the dough, in a blender, blend the chia seeds and water until smooth and thick.

In the bowl of a stand mixer fitted with the beater attachment, or using an electric handheld beater, combine the arrowroot, cashew butter, flaxseeds, coconut flour, coconut sugar, palm shortening, and baking powder. Add the thickened chia slurry and beat on high for 30 seconds until well incorporated. Let the dough sit for 5 minutes to allow the coconut flour to absorb some of the moisture, then mix again for 30 seconds. Gather the dough into a ball, then flatten it into a disk. Roll the dough out between two pieces of parchment paper to a ½-inch-thick oval.

To make the filling, in a small bowl, mix together the melted ghee, coconut sugar, honey, and cinnamon to make a thick paste. Spread the filling all over the rolled-out dough, then use the parchment paper to help roll the dough tightly, like a jelly roll. Gently seal the seam with your fingers, then reshape into a cylinder, if needed. Using a serrated knife, slice the log into 10 equal pieces each about 1½ inches thick. Place the cinnamon rolls, cut side up, in the prepared dish.

Bake for 40 minutes, or until golden on top and baked in the center. Cool for 20 minutes on a wire rack, then spread the whipped cream over the top so it melts slightly. Serve immediately or leave at room temperature for up to 2 hours.

make it ahead The dough can be made the night before and stored tightly wrapped, in the refrigerator. Bring to room temperature before rolling out. Alternatively, slightly under-bake the cinnamon rolls, cool completely, then wrap tightly and store in the freezer for up to 6 months. Defrost in the refrigerator overnight, then reheat in a 350°F oven for 10 to 15 minutes, until heated through. The whipped cream will keep in the refrigerator for up to 5 days.

sausage breakfast casserole

Holiday mornings are always a bit chaotic while last-minute preparations are being done, so I love to opt for make-ahead breakfasts. Prepare this the night before and pop it into the oven when you wake up.

SERVES 10

12 ounces sweet Italian sausage, casings removed and meat crumbled

2 cups shredded kale leaves (stems and center ribs discarded)

14 eggs

½ cup full-fat coconut milk

2 tablespoons chopped fresh basil

1 tablespoon chopped fresh flat-leaf parsley

1 teaspoon chopped fresh thyme

1 teaspoon fine sea salt

¼ teaspoon freshly ground black pepper

1 pound Hannah sweet potatoes or other white-fleshed variety, peeled and shredded

2 tomatoes, thinly sliced

Preheat the oven to 350°F.

In an oven-safe, shallow 5-quart braiser or 14-inch cast-iron skillet, cook the sausage over medium heat until browned and mostly cooked through, about 8 minutes. Add the kale and continue cooking for 5 minutes more, or until the kale is wilted. Remove the pan from the heat, drain the sausage mixture, discarding the grease, and return the sausage mixture to the pan.

In a large bowl, whisk together the eggs, coconut milk, basil, parsley, thyme, salt, and pepper. Stir in the sweet potatoes and pour the mixture into the pan with the sausage and kale. Place the tomato slices over the top of the casserole. Cover and bake in the oven for 30 minutes. Uncover and continue baking for 15 minutes, or until the center is set. Serve hot.

make it ahead Prepare the casserole up to 2 days in advance. Cover and store in the refrigerator until ready to bake.

tidbits Chicken, pork, turkey, or beef sausage can be used. Look for sausage that is nitrate-free and does not have additives or sugars. I like Hannah sweet potatoes for their mildly sweet white flesh, but any variety will do. Substitute celery root for the sweet potatoes for a lower carb dish.

If you tolerate dairy, mixing 1 cup grated Gruyère cheese in with the eggs takes this dish to the next level.

gingerbread latte

Serve this smooth and creamy coffee beverage with the flavors of gingerbread blended inside for a festive morning treat. Grind up some Gingersnap Cookies (page 307) to rim the mug, if desired.

SERVES 5

1 cup full-fat coconut milk

1 cup almond milk
(page 320)

¼ cup coconut sugar

2 tablespoons pure maple syrup

¾ teaspoon ground ginger

½ teaspoon ground cinnamon

¼ teaspoon ground nutmeg

¼ teaspoon ground cloves

5 cups strongly brewed coffee or espresso

Combine the coconut milk, almond milk, coconut sugar, maple syrup, ginger, cinnamon, nutmeg, and cloves in a saucepan and whisk over medium-high heat for 5 minutes. Stir in the coffee and, working in batches, add the mixture to a blender (or use an immersion blender) and blend until frothy, about 15 seconds. Serve immediately.

make it ahead To turn this into a coffee creamer, combine everything except the coffee. Stir the creamer into a hot cup of coffee or store it in the refrigerator in an airtight container for up to 1 week. To use the creamer in a single serving of latte, combine one part creamer to two parts coffee in a blender and blend until frothy.

tidbits For a truly classic gingerbread flavor, substitute unsulfured molasses for the maple syrup.

christmas dinner

menu

◆◆◆

*Persimmon
Prosciutto Salad*

Creamed Spinach

Vegetable Bacon Parcels

*Stuffing-Filled
Turkey Breast*

*Whole Roasted
Branzino with Fennel
and Tomatoes*

*Garlic Rosemary
Rib Roast*

◆◆◆

*Cranberry
Gingerbread Cake*

◆◆◆

Mulled Wine

My grandmother used to throw a big Christmas Eve party for more than fifty of our family members. She insisted on cooking the entire multi-course meal by herself, declining all help that was offered. She always made a few different proteins, a pasta dish, and more sides and desserts than you could count.

People have many different customs for Christmas Eve and Christmas dinner, so in an effort to give you a few alternatives for planning your menus, I've provided options for poultry, beef, and fish in this chapter. Choose the main dish that best fits with your own traditions and add one or two of the sides. You can even pull in some of your favorite sides from the Thanksgiving chapter. If you are anything like my grandmother, you will just make all of them, because she hates for anyone to miss out on their favorites!

Of course, you can cook a turkey (see page 249) or ham (see page 98) if that is a better fit for your family's tastes. Finish the meal with a cake full of seasonal flavors like gingerbread and cranberry, and warm your guests with a spicy mulled wine before they head out into the cold to journey home.

Merry Christmas!

persimmon prosciutto salad

Persimmons and a pomegranate vinaigrette give this salad festive color and flavor. I especially love the crunch from the pomegranate seeds and pumpkin seeds.

SERVES 10

6 ounces thinly sliced prosciutto, cut into ribbons

4 bunches watercress, thick stems trimmed

3 Fuyu persimmons, thinly sliced

½ cup pomegranate seeds

½ cup roasted pepitas (shelled pumpkin seeds)

dressing

½ cup extra-virgin olive oil

⅓ cup pure pomegranate juice

⅓ cup white wine vinegar

2 teaspoons light-colored raw honey

1 teaspoon Dijon mustard

Fine sea salt and freshly ground black pepper

Divide the prosciutto, watercress, persimmons, pomegranate seeds, and pepitas among 10 plates, or place all of the ingredients in a salad bowl and toss to combine.

To make the dressing, whisk together the olive oil, pomegranate juice, vinegar, honey, and mustard and season with salt and pepper. Drizzle 1 tablespoon of the dressing over each salad, or add ½ cup of the dressing to the salad bowl and toss to coat. Serve immediately with the extra dressing on the side.

tidbits Pure pomegranate juice can be found in most grocery stores.

creamed spinach

Creamed spinach used to be one of my and my dad's favorite holiday side dishes, but it was so full of dairy cream and cheese that I was always left feeling heavy. This version uses a garlic cashew cream sauce, and your guests will never know it's free of dairy.

SERVES 10

1 cup (about 150g) whole raw cashews

3 pounds spinach, stems trimmed

2 tablespoons ghee (page 325), extra-virgin olive oil or grass-fed unsalted butter

½ yellow onion, minced

4 cloves garlic, minced

1 cup water

1 teaspoon freshly squeezed lemon juice

1 teaspoon apple cider vinegar

1½ teaspoons fine sea salt

¼ teaspoon ground nutmeg

Place the cashews in a bowl and cover them with boiling water. Soak for 1 hour.

Bring a large pot of water to a boil and add the spinach. Cook until bright green and wilted, about 2 minutes. Pour the spinach into a colander and apply pressure to the top to remove all of the liquid. Transfer the spinach to a cutting board and coarsely chop it. If there's still a lot of liquid coming out, place a towel over the top and apply pressure to soak up any remaining water.

Heat the ghee in the same pot over medium-high heat. Add the onion and garlic and sauté for 5 minutes. Add the spinach and cook for 5 minutes more.

Meanwhile, drain the cashews and add them to a blender with the water, lemon juice, vinegar, salt, and nutmeg. Blend on high for about 1 minute, until very smooth.

Stir the cashew cream into the spinach mixture, then remove from the heat. Serve immediately.

make it ahead This dish can be made up to 3 days in advance and stored in an airtight container in the refrigerator. Return the mixture to a skillet over medium-low heat and stir until heated through.

vegetable bacon parcels

These pretty packages of vegetables tied up with smoky bacon are always a crowd-pleaser and look so festive on the table. Asher is known for unwrapping these and only eating the bacon, leaving the vegetables behind. But we're working on him!

SERVES 10

1 pound parsnips, peeled and cut into long spears

1 pound baby carrots, cleaned and trimmed

1 pound green beans, trimmed

1 tablespoon extra-virgin olive oil

10 slices thick-cut bacon

Fine sea salt and freshly ground black pepper

Preheat the oven to 425°F. Line a baking sheet with parchment paper.

Combine the parsnips, carrots, and green beans in a bowl and toss with the olive oil. Divide the vegetables into 10 bundles and wrap each tightly with a strip of bacon. Place the bundles, seam side down, on the prepared baking sheet. Sprinkle with salt and pepper.

Roast for 20 minutes, or until the vegetables are tender and the bacon is crisp. Transfer to a plate lined with paper towels to drain briefly, then remove the towels and serve hot.

make it ahead Assemble the parcels up to 2 days in advance and store in an airtight container in the refrigerator. Bring to room temperature prior to roasting.

stuffing-filled turkey breast

SERVES 10

4 cups blender bread (page 323), in ½-inch cubes

4 tablespoons melted ghee (page 325) or grass-fed unsalted butter

½ yellow onion, halved

1 large rib celery, halved

2 cloves garlic, peeled

2 sprigs thyme

2 fresh sage leaves

1 sprig rosemary

1 sprig flat-leaf parsley

1 cup whole jarred chestnuts

2 eggs, whisked

½ cup turkey or chicken stock (page 327)

1½ teaspoons fine sea salt, plus more to season

¼ teaspoon freshly ground black pepper, plus more to season

1 turkey breast (about 5½ pounds), skin on, boned, trimmed, and butterflied

pan gravy

½ yellow onion

½ garlic head, cloves unpeeled

2 cups turkey or chicken stock (page 327), plus more if needed

2 tablespoons melted ghee (page 325) or grass-fed unsalted butter

Fine sea salt and freshly ground black pepper, to season

½ cup (about 70g) whole raw cashews, soaked in boiling water for 1 hour

Here, a turkey breast is filled with a chestnut bread stuffing, rolled up, roasted, and then served with a pan gravy. A dollop of homemade Cranberry Sauce (page 238) would be fantastic on top, as well. Ask your butcher to butterfly the breast, which involves splitting the meat almost in half so it will lie flat and roll easily.

Preheat the oven to 375°F.

Toss the bread in 2 tablespoons of the ghee and spread evenly on a baking sheet. Toast the bread cubes for 15 minutes, stirring once for even browning. Set aside.

Combine the onion, celery, garlic, thyme, sage, rosemary, parsley, and chestnuts in a food processor. Pulse 6 to 8 times, until everything is finely chopped.

Heat the remaining 2 tablespoons ghee in a large skillet over medium heat. Pour the vegetables into the pan and sauté for 10 minutes. Remove from the heat and stir in the bread cubes, eggs, turkey stock, salt, and pepper.

Place the turkey breast on the cutting board with the skin side down and the longest side nearest you. If needed, pound it with a meat tenderizer or rolling pin to create an even surface. Season generously with salt and pepper. Spread the stuffing on top, leaving a 1-inch border on the long side, and roll the turkey up like a jelly roll. Be careful not to roll it too tightly or the stuffing will seep out of the ends. Wrap kitchen twine around the breast crosswise and tie tightly to hold the roll in place. Place the turkey in a roasting pan.

To make the pan gravy, add the onion half, half garlic head, and 1 cup of the turkey stock to the roasting pan. Drizzle with the melted ghee and season with salt and pepper. Roast for 50 to 60 minutes, basting with the pan juices every 20 minutes during cooking, until the internal temperature of the center of the turkey breast is 165°F.

Transfer the turkey to a cutting board and tent it with aluminum foil. Let the turkey rest for 15 minutes while you finish the gravy.

CONTINUED

stuffing-filled turkey breast, continued

Place the roasted onion half in a blender and squeeze the garlic cloves out of their skins into the blender. While the pan is still hot, whisk in the remaining 1 cup stock to release any browned bits from the bottom. Pour the liquid through a sieve into the blender. Drain and rinse the cashews and add half of them to the blender. Blend until very smooth. Add the remaining cashews if the gravy is not thick enough; add a little extra stock if too thick. Season with more salt and pepper. (Warm the gravy in a saucepan over low heat if necessary.)

Snip off the kitchen twine and slice the turkey breast into ½-inch-thick pieces. Arrange decoratively on a platter and serve warm with the gravy on the side.

make it ahead Prepare the stuffing up to 2 days in advance. The uncooked rolled turkey can be stored, tightly wrapped, in the refrigerator for up to 12 hours. Roast the turkey and make the gravy up to 2 hours before serving. Pour 2 cups of the gravy onto the bottom of a serving platter and arrange the turkey slices on top. Cover and leave at room temperature for up to 2 hours, then reheat, covered, in a 350°F oven for 15 minutes.

whole roasted branzino with fennel and tomatoes

Italian Christmas celebrations, or at least the Italian American Christmas Eve I grew up with, always include a fish entrée in addition to the beef or poultry. My grandmother makes salmon because it is her favorite, but I love to prepare a whole Mediterranean fish like branzino. Its mild flavor and simple preparation even appeal to those who do not love fish. If you are serving only this dish as the main course, you may want to double the recipe.

SERVES 4 TO 6

2 branzino (European sea bass), scaled and gutted with head and tail intact, 1 to 1½ pounds each

Fine sea salt

4 sprigs rosemary

1 lemon, sliced into 4 rounds

4 tablespoons extra-virgin olive oil or melted ghee (page 325)

2 tablespoons chopped fresh flat-leaf parsley

Freshly ground black pepper

2 small fennel bulbs

1 cup cherry tomatoes, halved

4 cloves garlic, thinly sliced

Preheat the oven to 425°F.

Rinse the fish and pat dry with paper towels. Using a sharp knife, make slashes on both sides of the fish, cutting down to the bone. Season the branzino cavities with salt and stuff each cavity with 2 rosemary sprigs and 2 lemon pieces. In a small bowl, stir together 3 tablespoons of the olive oil and parsley and season with salt and pepper. Rub the mixture all over the outside of the fish.

Remove the stems and feathery fronds from the fennel bulbs. Cut the bulbs in half lengthwise and then into thin slices. Toss with the remaining 1 tablespoon olive oil, the tomatoes, and the garlic and season with salt and pepper. Spread the vegetables in a roasting pan in a thin layer. Place the fish on top.

Bake for 20 to 30 minutes, until the flesh is opaque when cut near the bone and the fennel and tomatoes are tender.

Transfer the fish to a warmed platter and scatter the fennel and tomatoes around the dish. Spoon the pan juices over the top of the fish and serve.

tidbits Branzino has delicately flavored white flesh. Striped bass or red snapper would also be great prepared this way.

Ask your fishmonger to gut and clean the fish for you.

garlic rosemary rib roast

In my dad's family, it was traditional to make this classic roast every Christmas. Although we lived far away from his family when I was growing up, he took pride in carrying on his mom's custom of making a rib roast, which gave my mom a little break from the kitchen.

SERVES 10

1 (7-pound) standing rib roast of beef, fat trimmed and tied with twine

10 cloves garlic, peeled and sliced

2 teaspoons arrowroot powder

6 sprigs rosemary

6 tablespoons ghee (page 325) or extra-virgin olive oil

Fine sea salt and freshly ground black pepper

1 to 2 cups beef or chicken stock (page 327)

1 yellow onion, diced

tidbits Save the bones for beef stock (page 327).

Preheat the oven to 450°F. Poke shallow holes with a sharp knife all over the roast and insert the garlic slices into the holes. Rub all over with the arrowroot powder and tuck the rosemary sprigs into the twine on the top and bottom of the roast.

Melt 4 tablespoons of the ghee over medium-high heat in a large skillet or Dutch oven. Sear the roast on all sides, then transfer it to a roasting pan and return the skillet to the stove. Season the roast generously on all sides with salt and pepper and pour in 1 cup of the beef stock. Roast in the oven for 20 minutes.

Meanwhile, add the remaining 2 tablespoons ghee to the same skillet. Add the onion and sauté for about 10 minutes, until well browned.

Reduce the oven temperature to 350°F, spoon the sautéed onion over the roast, return the pan to the oven, and continue roasting, basting with the pan juices every 30 minutes, for 1½ to 2 hours, until an instant-read thermometer inserted into the center of the roast reads about 140°F for medium doneness. If the liquid in the pan nearly evaporates, add the remaining 1 cup stock.

Remove the twine, cover the roast with foil, and allow it to rest for 30 minutes before slicing. Set the roast on its side and run a sharp knife between the bones and meat; remove the bones and set them aside. Turn the roast right side up. Carve the roast into slices ¼ to ½ inch thick and arrange on a platter. Spoon the pan juices over the top. Serve immediately.

make it ahead Prep the garlic and onion up to 3 days in advance and store in an airtight container in the refrigerator. Ready the roast in the pan the night before, wrap tightly, and refrigerate. Roast the beef up to 2 hours before serving, slice, pour the pan juices onto an oven-safe platter, and top with the beef slices. Cover tightly, leave at room temperature for up to 2 hours, then reheat in a 350°F oven for 15 to 20 minutes. The juices will help steam the meat and keep it moist during reheating.

cranberry gingerbread cake

This layer cake uses all of my favorite flavors—gingerbread, dark chocolate, tart cranberries—and makes an impressive ending to a Christmas dinner.

SERVES 10

8 ounces fresh cranberries

1¼ cups pure maple syrup

¼ cup palm shortening, ghee (page 325), or grass-fed unsalted butter

½ cup coconut sugar

4 eggs

¾ cup unsweetened almond butter

¼ cup coconut flour

2 tablespoons natural cocoa powder

1 tablespoon ground ginger

Finely grated zest of 1 lemon

2½ teaspoons freshly squeezed lemon juice

1 teaspoon pure vanilla extract

1 teaspoon baking soda

½ teaspoon ground cinnamon

¼ teaspoon fine sea salt

¼ teaspoon ground cardamom

Whipped cream (page 332) or whipped coconut cream (page 331), for serving

Preheat the oven to 350°F. Lightly grease two 6 by 3-inch cake pans with coconut oil and fit round pieces of parchment paper into each pan.

To make the compote, combine the cranberries and 1 cup of the maple syrup in a small saucepan over medium-high heat and cook for 10 minutes, or until the berries have popped. Mash them slightly with the back of a spoon. Remove from the heat and set aside.

In a small saucepan over medium heat, melt the palm shortening with the remaining ¼ cup maple syrup and the coconut sugar for about 10 minutes, until the mixture is completely liquid. Set aside to cool.

Add the eggs, almond butter, coconut flour, cocoa powder, ginger, lemon zest and juice, vanilla, baking soda, cinnamon, salt, and cardamom to a blender or food processor. Blend for 30 seconds on high speed, or until fully combined. Add the melted mixture and blend on high speed for 30 seconds more, or until smooth. Divide the batter between the prepared pans.

Reserve half of the cranberry compote for the topping. Drop bits of the remaining compote all around the pans, then swirl in with a knife until mostly incorporated. Bake for 20 minutes, or until a toothpick inserted into the center of the cakes comes out clean. Cool on a wire rack for 30 minutes, then use a knife to gently release the cakes from the sides of the pans. Turn the pans over to release the cakes and cool completely, right side up, on the rack. Layer the cakes with the whipped cream. Serve additional cranberry compote on top of the cake.

make it ahead Make the compote up to 5 days in advance and store in an airtight container in the refrigerator.

Make the cake up to 3 days in advance. Store the layers, tightly wrapped in parchment paper and then plastic wrap, in the refrigerator. Bring to room temperature before layering with whipped cream.

tidbits See Tidbits (page 152) for how to bake one 9-inch cake or 12 cupcakes.

mulled wine

My sister-in-law brought this delicious tradition to the family. I like to say its Napa's version of a hot toddy, even though it is of old-world heritage. Red wine is simmered with cider-friendly spices and served warm for any festive holiday celebration. Any of your favorite Cabernets, Syrahs, or Petit Syrahs will work well.

SERVES 8

32 whole cloves

2 navel oranges, cut crosswise into 8 slices and slices halved

24 allspice berries

4 star anise

3 cinnamon sticks

3 (750-ml) bottles red wine

¾ cup coconut sugar

Pinch of fine sea salt

Stick 2 cloves into the peel of each half orange slice. Place the allspice, star anise, and cinnamon sticks on a piece of cheesecloth, tie into a bundle, and set aside.

Pour the wine into a large pot set over low heat. Stir in the coconut sugar and salt until dissolved. Add the orange slices and spice bundle and steep for 1 hour to allow the flavors to develop.

Ladle into mugs and garnish each with a clove-studded orange slice.

menu

❖❖❖

Granny Sarella's Panettone

Gingerbread House

Thumbprint Cookies

Sunbutter Buckeyes

Gingersnap Cookies

Granny Sarella's Biscotti

Cutout Cookies

Christmas Fudge

❖❖❖

Peppermint Hot Cocoa

Marshmallows

Eggnog

christmas treats

What would Christmastime be without all of the seasonal treats? For some people, this is the tastiest part of the season. My sister, mom, and I spend a day or two every December watching Christmas movies and baking dozens of treats. We package them up to give as gifts and we take a few dozen to our annual cookie exchange.

You'll find healthful re-creations of classics like gingersnaps, fudge, and cutout sugar cookies in the pages that follow. Build (and even nibble on!) a grain-free gingerbread house, or make homemade marshmallows to float in peppermint hot cocoa. And after years of receiving requests from readers for a grain-free biscotti recipe, I have included one that I converted from an heirloom family recipe.

Happy holiday baking!

granny sarella's panettone

One of the most popular recipes from my first cookbook, *Against All Grain*, has been my great-grandmother's spaghetti sauce recipe. This recipe for her panettone is destined to become another favorite. I had to create a grain-free version so I could continue baking it each season for my family. Without the presence of yeast and gluten, this is a little more dense than the traditional airy panettone, but the flavors are just like I remember, and it is delightful toasted and topped with ghee and jam.

SERVES 10

5 eggs, separated

½ teaspoon cream of tartar

½ cup coconut sugar

½ cup palm shortening, melted

½ cup almond milk (page 320)

¼ cup whiskey or brandy (see Tidbits)

3¼ cups blanched almond flour

1 cup arrowroot powder

2 tablespoons coconut flour

1½ teaspoons fine sea salt

1 teaspoon baking soda

1 teaspoon grain-free baking powder (page 325)

Finely grated zest of 1 lemon

Finely grated zest of 1 orange

½ cup raisins

Preheat the oven to 350°F. Place a 6¾-inch panettone mold on a baking sheet, or grease the inside of a round casserole dish similar in size.

Using a stand mixer fitted with the whisk attachment, or using an electric handheld beater, beat the egg whites with the cream of tartar until soft peaks form. Transfer the whites to a separate bowl and set aside.

Beat the egg yolks with the coconut sugar and palm shortening on medium speed for 30 seconds. Add the almond milk and whiskey and beat again to incorporate. Add the almond flour, arrowroot, coconut flour, salt, baking soda, baking powder, lemon zest, and orange zest and beat on medium-high for 30 seconds, or until well incorporated. Stir in the raisins, then gently fold in the beaten egg whites. Pour the batter into the prepared baking mold and gently smooth the top.

Bake for 60 to 65 minutes, until golden and puffed up on top and a toothpick inserted into the center of the loaf comes out clean. Cool completely on a wire rack before serving or storing. Remove from the mold, slice, and serve as is or toasted.

make it ahead Store the baked panettone, tightly wrapped in parchment paper and then plastic wrap, in the refrigerator for up to 1 week or in the freezer for up to 6 months. Defrost overnight in the refrigerator.

tidbits Substitute 3 tablespoons fresh orange juice plus 2 teaspoons vanilla extract for the alcohol, if desired.

gingerbread house

This grain-free version of one of my favorite seasonal pastimes makes it possible for anyone with allergies to enjoy baking, decorating, and eating his or her own homemade gingerbread house. Asher is obsessed with gingerbread making, and by the end of the season, we usually have a whole gingerbread village on the bookshelf! Download the gingerbread house templates at CelebrationsCookbook.com/gingerbread-house to start your own village.

MAKES 1 GINGERBREAD HOUSE

gingerbread

3 cups blanched almond flour

¾ cup arrowroot powder

1 tablespoon coconut flour

1 tablespoon ground cinnamon

1 tablespoon ground ginger

1 teaspoon ground cloves

1 teaspoon baking soda

½ cup palm shortening, (see Tidbits, page 301)

½ cup coconut sugar

¼ cup pure maple syrup

1 egg

royal icing

2 egg whites

3 cups confectioners' sugar

1 teaspoon pure vanilla extract

Naturally colored, gluten-free candies, for decorating (optional)

To make the gingerbread, sift together the almond flour, arrowroot, coconut flour, cinnamon, ginger, cloves, and baking soda into a bowl.

In the bowl of a stand mixer fitted with the beater attachment, or using an electric handheld mixer, cream the palm shortening, coconut sugar, and maple syrup on medium speed for 1 minute, or until light and fluffy. Add the egg and mix again on medium speed until combined. Add the dry mix to the stand mixer and beat on high until the ingredients are fully combined and a dough forms.

Remove the dough from the bowl and divide in half. Form each half into a ball, flatten the balls into disks, and wrap each disk tightly in plastic wrap. Chill for 2 hours.

Preheat the oven to 375°F. Line a baking sheet with parchment paper. Trace the house template onto parchment paper and cut out the pieces.

Remove 1 disk of dough from the refrigerator and roll it out to ¼-inch thickness between two pieces of parchment paper. Cut out as many template shapes as you can from the dough. Slide the paper onto the prepared baking sheet, spacing the pieces out slightly. Gather the remaining dough and place it in the refrigerator to chill again while you work with the second disk.

Bake the first set of shapes for 10 to 12 minutes, until set. Repeat with the remaining dough and template shapes. Use any extra dough for gingerbread people or trees. Cool the gingerbread on a wire rack before decorating and putting the house together.

CONTINUED

gingerbread house, continued

To make the royal icing, in the stand mixer fitted with the whisk attachment, or using an electric handheld mixer, beat the egg whites with the confectioners' sugar on medium speed for 7 to 10 minutes, until the icing is thick enough to hold its shape. Stir in the vanilla extract.

Assemble the dough pieces, except the roof, to build the house, using the royal icing to seal all of the seams. Prop the walls up with cans if needed until the frosting dries, about 30 minutes. Place the roof pieces on last, after the house structure has dried and set. Decorate to your liking with candy.

tidbits Unsulfured molasses can be substituted for the maple syrup for a more classic gingerbread flavor.

While not Paleo, royal icing must be used to hold the house together. To make gingerbread for eating, use any of my Paleo-friendly frostings for decorating. Many health food stores have candies that do not have artificial coloring or flavorings and are gluten-free for decorating; plain leaf gelatin sheets make lovely windows.

To substitute unsalted grass-fed butter for the palm shortening, reduce the amount to ⅓ cup.

thumbprint cookies

These easy shortbread cookies filled with sweet jam make lovely gifts. The cookies are egg-free if you omit the optional egg wash.

6 tablespoons ghee (page 325), palm shortening, or grass-fed unsalted butter

⅓ cup light-colored raw honey

¼ teaspoon pure vanilla extract

1½ cups blanched almond flour

½ cup coconut flour

1 egg (optional)

1 tablespoon water (optional)

Unsweetened shredded coconut or sliced almonds (optional)

¼ cup fruit-sweetened jam

Preheat the oven to 350°F. Line a baking sheet with parchment paper.

In the bowl of a stand mixer fitted with the beater attachment, or using an electric handheld mixer, beat together the ghee, honey, and vanilla on medium-high speed for 1 minute, or until smooth and fluffy. With the mixer on low speed, add the almond and coconut flours and mix just until incorporated.

Shape the dough into 1-inch balls, using about 2 tablespoons of dough for each. Place on the prepared baking sheets, spacing them evenly apart. If desired, make the egg wash by beating together the egg and water. Roll the dough balls in the egg wash and then in the shredded coconut.

Moisten your thumb with water and gently press into the center of each ball, making an indentation about ½ inch wide and 1 inch deep. Spoon about 1 teaspoon jam into each indentation.

Bake the cookies for 15 to 17 minutes, until golden. Transfer to a wire rack and let cool completely.

make it ahead Store the cookies in an airtight container in the refrigerator for up to 1 week. To freeze, wrap the baking sheet of unbaked cookies tightly with plastic wrap and freeze in a single layer. Once frozen, place the cookies in an airtight container and freeze for up to 6 months. Remove the desired amount of cookies from the freezer and defrost overnight in the refrigerator. Bake as directed.

sunbutter buckeyes

Each year, my grandma Marge hosts a cookie exchange, and in past years, her peanut butter buckeyes were always the first thing to be eaten off the plate that I took home. Here, I use sunflower butter to keep these cookies both nut- and legume-free, and the no-bake peanut butter-flavored fudge is rolled into balls and dipped in a homemade chocolate coating that's free from refined sugar, soy, or dairy. This is one of my favorite holiday treats.

MAKES 18 COOKIES

sunbutter filling

½ cup sunflower seed butter

¼ cup pure maple syrup

2 tablespoons plus 1 teaspoon coconut flour

2 tablespoons arrowroot powder

1 teaspoon pure vanilla extract

¼ teaspoon fine sea salt

chocolate shell

3 ounces raw cacao butter, chopped

2½ tablespoons pure maple syrup

⅓ cup plus 1 tablespoon natural cocoa powder

Pinch of fine sea salt

¼ teaspoon pure vanilla extract

Line a baking sheet with parchment paper.

To make the filling, combine the sunflower seed butter, maple syrup, coconut flour, arrowroot powder, vanilla, and salt and mix well. Set aside for 2 minutes for the coconut flour to absorb and expand. With a small scoop or spoon, shape eighteen 1-inch balls and place them on the prepared baking sheet, spacing them evenly apart. Put the baking sheet with the sunbutter balls in the freezer to harden.

Meanwhile, make the chocolate shell. Heat 2 inches of water in a saucepan over medium heat until just barely simmering. In a glass bowl that fits inside the saucepan without touching the simmering water, add the cacao butter and whisk constantly for about 15 minutes, until the cacao butter is fully melted and registers 105°F on a candy thermometer.

Turn off the heat and carefully remove the glass bowl from the saucepan. Adding one ingredient at a time, gently whisk in the maple syrup, cocoa powder, salt, and vanilla and whisk until just combined. Switch to a rubber spatula and gently stir until the mixture has cooled. The chocolate should be smooth and shiny and have a slightly thickened liquid consistency. Set aside.

Pull the sunbutter balls out of the freezer. Stick a toothpick into the top of a sunbutter ball and dip the ball into the chocolate shell mixture until it is almost fully covered, leaving an exposed circle of filling at the top. Repeat with the remaining sunbutter balls. Place them in the fridge to harden for 20 minutes. Serve immediately, or store in the refrigerator in an airtight container for up to 2 weeks.

tidbit If making homemade chocolate seems daunting, simply melt 4 ounces dark chocolate of your choice.

gingersnap cookies

These gingersnaps have a fabulous spicy ginger taste and a good crisp texture. Instead of using the traditional molasses, as it can be difficult for some people to digest, I caramelize honey and low-glycemic coconut sugar to give these cookies that deep molasses flavor.

MAKES 12 COOKIES

- ¼ cup light-colored raw honey *[½]*
- 2 tablespoons coconut sugar *[4]*
- 2 tablespoons ghee (page 325), palm shortening, or grass-fed unsalted butter *[4]*
- ¼ teaspoon pure vanilla extract *[½]*
- 1 cup cashew flour (see Tidbits) *[2]*
- ¼ cup arrowroot powder *[½]*
- 1 tablespoon coconut flour *[2]*
- 2 teaspoons ground ginger *[4]*
- ¼ teaspoon ground cinnamon *[½]*
- ¼ teaspoon ground nutmeg *[½]*
- ½ teaspoon baking soda *[1]*

Preheat the oven to 350°F.

Heat the honey in a saucepan over medium-high heat. Once it starts to bubble, turn down the heat to low and simmer for 5 minutes, or until the honey turns a dark amber color. Add the coconut sugar and continue to simmer for 2 minutes longer. Remove from the heat and whisk in the ghee and vanilla extract.

Combine the cashew flour, arrowroot powder, coconut flour, ginger, cinnamon, nutmeg, and baking soda in a food processor. Process for 1 minute. Pour in the melted ingredients and process again for 30 seconds, or until a dough forms.

Shape the dough into a ball with your hands, then roll it out to a ¼-inch thickness between two pieces of parchment paper. Use a 2-inch round cookie cutter to cut circles, then peel away the excess dough. Reroll the dough scraps and repeat cutting out cookies until all of the dough is used. Transfer the bottom sheet of parchment paper with the cookies onto a baking sheet.

Bake for 8 to 10 minutes, until browned and crisp around the edges. Cool completely on wire racks before eating.

make it ahead The cookies can be made up to 2 days in advance and stored in an airtight container in the refrigerator. They will lose some crispness after that.

tidbits Blanched almond flour or finely ground raw sunflower seeds will work instead of cashew flour, if desired. Omit the baking soda if using sunflower flour.

granny sarella's biscotti

My grandma has been making batches of her mom's biscotti recipes to give as gifts ever since I can remember. Sometimes she even dips one end in a little melted chocolate for an extra-special treat. Biscotti is one of the most requested recipe makeovers from my readers, so I asked my grandma for her recipe to re-create, and finally created a cookie that I am pleased to share with all of you.

MAKES 36 BISCOTTI

½ cup palm shortening, softened (see Tidbits)

¾ cup coconut sugar

¼ cup pure maple syrup

3 eggs

1 teaspoon grain-free baking powder (page 325)

1 teaspoon freshly squeezed lemon juice

½ teaspoon almond extract

¼ teaspoon fine sea salt

2½ cups cashew flour (see Tidbits)

1½ cups arrowroot powder

¼ cup plus 2 tablespoons coconut flour

½ cup sliced almonds

Preheat the oven to 350°F. Line a baking sheet with parchment paper.

In the bowl of a stand mixer fitted with the beater attachment, or using an electric handheld mixer, cream together the palm shortening, coconut sugar, and maple syrup on medium speed for 1 minute. Add the eggs, one at a time, beating after each addition, until fully incorporated. Scrape down the sides of the bowl. Add the baking powder, lemon juice, almond extract, and salt to the bowl and mix to combine. Add the cashew flour, arrowroot, and coconut flour and mix on medium speed to incorporate. Let the dough rest for 15 minutes, then beat again for 30 seconds.

Divide the dough in half, form each half into a 4 by 11-inch loaf that's 1½ inches thick, and place on the prepared baking sheet. Sprinkle the almonds on top of each loaf and slightly press down to ensure they are stuck to the loaf.

Bake for 25 minutes. Remove from the oven, leaving the heat on. Allow the loaves to cool for 10 minutes. Then, with a sharp knife, cut the loaves diagonally into 1-inch-thick slices. Place the slices flat on the baking sheet and bake for an additional 10 minutes. Reduce the oven temperature to 250°F. Bake for 25 minutes longer, flipping the cookies once halfway through, until crisp and golden.

Remove from the oven and cool completely on a wire rack.

make it ahead Store in an airtight container in the refrigerator for up 2 weeks or in the freezer for up to 6 months.

tidbits Blanched almond flour can be substituted for the cashew flour, if desired.

To substitute unsalted grass-fed butter for the palm shortening, reduce the amount to ⅓ cup.

cutout cookies

These buttery cookies are soft and chewy and can be used year-round for any holiday celebrations. To make frostings of different colors, look for dye-free food coloring in your local health food store or online.

MAKES 12 COOKIES

2½ cups blanched almond flour

2 teaspoons arrowroot powder

¼ cup light-colored raw honey

1 egg

2 teaspoons coconut oil

½ teaspoon pure vanilla extract

½ teaspoon baking soda

¼ teaspoon fine sea salt

frosting

6 tablespoons coconut butter

1 ounce raw cacao butter, chopped

¼ cup light-colored raw honey

¼ cup chilled full-fat coconut milk

Natural food coloring (optional)

Preheat the oven to 350°F. Line a baking sheet with parchment paper.

Combine the almond flour, arrowroot, honey, egg, coconut oil, vanilla, baking soda, and salt in a food processor and process until a smooth ball forms, about 30 seconds. Flatten the ball of dough into a ½-inch-thick disk and wrap in plastic wrap. Chill in the refrigerator for 20 minutes.

Place the dough between two sheets of parchment paper and roll out to ¼-inch thickness. Remove the top parchment sheet. Dip a cookie cutter in a little flour, then cut out shapes, peeling away the excess dough. Gather the excess dough into a ball and reroll it to make more cookies. If the dough starts to dry out or crack when rolled the second time, lightly moisten your hands before kneading the scraps to add a little moisture back into the dough. Place the cookies on the prepared baking sheet, spacing them evenly.

Bake for 8 to 10 minutes, until golden around the edges. Cool completely on a wire rack.

Meanwhile, make the frosting. Combine the coconut butter and cacao butter in a saucepan over low heat until melted, but not boiling. Pour into a food processor and add the honey and coconut milk. Process until smooth and combined. Pour the frosting into a bowl and chill in the refrigerator for 20 minutes to set. Divide the frosting into small bowls and add food coloring, if desired. Pipe designs or spread the frosting onto the cooled cookies.

make it ahead The dough can be chilled in the refrigerator for up to 2 days. Baked cookies can be frozen, unfrosted, in an airtight container for up to 6 months. Defrost in the refrigerator overnight. Frost these cookies right before serving because the cookie tends to absorb some of the oils from the frosting if stored too long.

christmas fudge

Every year at Christmastime, my mom and grandma used to make fudge to give away as gifts or take to all of the holiday cookie exchanges. As I started to think about how to re-create that memory and a new recipe, I asked my mom if she had a copy of the recipe my grandma used. Turns out it was the one from the back of the marshmallow fluff jar! Instead of going through the trouble of making homemade marshmallows, then turning them into fudge, I came up with a simple recipe of just eight ingredients. Its flavor and texture are similar to the fudge I remember. There's no candy thermometer required, and it only uses one pot.

MAKES 24 FUDGE SQUARES

1 cup pure maple syrup

½ cup coconut sugar

¼ cup expeller-pressed coconut oil or ghee (page 325)

1 cup raw cashew butter

6 tablespoons arrowroot powder

2 teaspoons pure vanilla extract

½ teaspoon fine sea salt

12 ounces unsweetened baking chocolate (100 percent cacao), chopped

Line a 9 by 13-inch baking dish with parchment paper and leave flaps hanging over the side of the dish for easy removal.

In a saucepan over medium-low heat, combine the maple syrup, coconut sugar, and coconut oil. Stir until the coconut sugar melts and the mixture is liquid, about 5 minutes. Whisk in the cashew butter, arrowroot powder, vanilla, salt, and chocolate and continue stirring over low heat until the chocolate melts and everything is well blended, about 5 minutes more.

Pour the fudge into the prepared baking dish and smooth the top with a rubber spatula. Chill in the refrigerator until set, about 6 hours. Cut into squares and serve.

make it ahead Once the fudge has cooled to room temperature, cover the pan tightly with plastic wrap and store in the refrigerator for up to 2 weeks or in the freezer for up to 3 months. Thaw in the refrigerator overnight before cutting into squares and serving.

peppermint hot cocoa

Growing up in Colorado, I spent a lot of time playing out in the snow. Afterward, when I went inside, I would always warm up with a mug of hot cocoa. Those days it was straight from the packet with boiling water, but this dairy-free version uses a mixture of rich dark chocolate and cocoa powder to make a thick drinking chocolate. We drink it every year now while we decorate the house for Christmas, or when we visit the mountains so Asher can see snow. He prefers his without the peppermint, so I ladle his out before adding it. Top with gooey Marshmallows (page 316), or add coffee to turn this into a peppermint mocha (see Tidbits, below).

SERVES 4

2 cups almond milk (page 320)

1 (13.5-ounce) can full-fat coconut milk, or 1½ cups cashew milk (page 324)

3 ounces dark chocolate (85 percent cacao), chopped

2 tablespoons natural cocoa powder

½ cup pure maple syrup or raw honey

½ teaspoon peppermint extract

Combine the almond milk and coconut milk in a saucepan over medium-high heat and heat for 5 minutes. Turn the heat to low and whisk in the chocolate, cocoa powder, and maple syrup. Heat for about 5 minutes, whisking occasionally, until the chocolate melts and the mixture is thick and creamy. Stir in the peppermint extract, remove from the heat, and pour into mugs to serve.

make it ahead Store in an airtight container in the refrigerator for up to 1 week and reheat over medium heat.

tidbits To make a peppermint mocha, place 1 cup coffee and ½ cup of the peppermint cocoa per serving in a blender and blend on medium speed for 30 seconds, or until frothy.

marshmallows

These have the same texture and flavor you remember from childhood but without the corn syrup and refined sugar. They melt into a sweet gooey puddle in your hot cocoa or morning cup of coffee, and can even be dipped in the chocolate shell recipe (see page 304) for chocolate-covered marshmallows.

MAKES 24 LARGE MARSHMALLOWS

2 to 3 tablespoons arrowroot powder, for coating

1 cup water

3 tablespoons unflavored gelatin powder

1 cup light-colored raw honey

1 teaspoon pure vanilla extract

Line a baking sheet with parchment paper and spread 1 tablespoon of the arrowroot evenly over the parchment to cover.

Into the bowl of a stand mixer fitted with the whisk attachment, or using an electric handheld mixer, pour ½ cup of the water and sprinkle the gelatin over the top. Allow the gelatin to bloom, or absorb the water, for 10 minutes.

Combine the remaining ½ cup water and the honey in a saucepan. Bring to a boil over medium-high heat and boil for 15 minutes, or until a candy thermometer reads 240°F.

Turn the mixer on low, and with it running, slowly pour the hot honey syrup down the side of the bowl. Add the vanilla, then increase the speed of the mixer to medium-high and beat for 8 to 10 minutes. The mixture will turn from brown to white and triple in volume.

Turn the marshmallow crème out onto the prepared baking sheet and smooth it with an offset spatula. You need to work quickly here, before the marshmallow starts to set. Allow the crème to cool and set at room temperature for 6 hours.

Rub the top of the marshmallows all over with 1 tablespoon of the arrowroot powder. Lightly grease a sharp knife with coconut oil and slice the marshmallow into 24 pieces. If the marshmallows are still sticky, toss the pieces gently in the remaining 1 tablespoon arrowroot to coat them. Serve immediately.

make it ahead Store in an airtight container at room temperature for up to 2 weeks.

eggnog

This is a refined sugar-free alternative to a favorite winter treat. Drink it straight from the fridge, spike it for a little holiday spirit, or add a splash of the mixture to your morning coffee.

SERVES 4

1 (13.5-ounce) can full-fat coconut milk

6 whole cloves

3 egg yolks

¼ cup pure maple syrup or light-colored raw honey

1 teaspoon pure vanilla extract

½ teaspoon ground nutmeg

¼ teaspoon ground cinnamon

1 cup cashew milk (page 324)

Rum, brandy, or bourbon, for spiking (optional)

Ground nutmeg, for garnish

Heat the coconut milk and cloves in a saucepan over medium-high heat for 5 minutes.

Whisk together the egg yolks, maple syrup, vanilla, nutmeg, and cinnamon in a bowl. Slowly pour the hot coconut milk into the bowl, whisking continuously. Return the liquid to the pan and cook over medium-low heat for 5 minutes, stirring continuously. Do not let it boil.

Pour the eggnog through a fine-mesh sieve into a glass container and whisk in the cashew milk. Cover and refrigerate until chilled completely, about 4 hours.

Add a splash of alcohol of choice to each serving, if desired, and garnish with nutmeg.

make it ahead Store the eggnog in an airtight container in the refrigerator for up to 5 days.

the basics

If you are new to following a grain-free and Paleo lifestyle, it may come as a bit of a shock to realize that you have to make condiments you're used to picking up at the store and spend days at a time on activities like simmering chicken stock. I make a lot of these basic items from scratch not only because they taste better, but also because the store-bought versions contain refined sugars or preservatives that are not in keeping with my diet. I spend one day on the weekend prepping these items so I can use them throughout the week, but there are also a lot of Paleo-friendly brands starting to show up on the market, so keep an eye out for those as well. (I've included my favorite brands for some shortcut items in the Ingredients Glossary and Substitutions section on page 12.)

MAKES 4 CUPS

1 cup raw almonds

8 cups filtered water

¼ teaspoon fine sea salt

almond milk

This version is unsweetened and can be used for any of my recipes that call for almond milk. To substitute store-bought almond milk, purchase the unsweetened original flavor and look for brands with the fewest ingredients and no carrageenan or gums.

Combine the almonds in a bowl with 4 cups of the water and ⅛ teaspoon of the salt and soak for at least 10 hours or up to overnight.

Drain the nuts and rinse well. Transfer them to a blender and fill with the remaining 4 cups water. Add the remaining ⅛ teaspoon salt and puree until smooth.

Strain the milk through a fine-mesh sieve, a nut milk bag, or doubled cheesecloth. Squeeze to remove all of the liquid. Serve immediately or store in an airtight container in the refrigerator for up to 5 days.

tidbits If you plan to drink the almond milk on its own or use it for a sweet dish, add 1 to 3 pitted dates to the blender to sweeten it naturally.

Other nuts can be substituted for the almonds to make a variety of nut milks. Try hazelnuts, walnuts, or pecans for a fresh spin on this dairy-free milk alternative! For cashew milk, see page 324.

3 ounces pitted dates

2 cups tomato puree

¼ cup water

½ cup apple cider vinegar

¼ cup tomato paste

2 tablespoons coconut aminos

2 teaspoons fish sauce

1½ teaspoons natural liquid smoke

1 teaspoon fine sea salt

1 teaspoon sweet paprika

1 teaspoon chili powder

1 teaspoon Dijon mustard

½ teaspoon cayenne pepper

½ teaspoon minced garlic

½ teaspoon onion powder

½ teaspoon ground allspice

½ teaspoon freshly ground black pepper

barbecue sauce

Soak the dates in warm water to cover for 15 minutes, then drain.

Combine the dates with the tomato puree, water, vinegar, tomato paste, coconut aminos, fish sauce, liquid smoke, salt, paprika, chili powder, mustard, cayenne, garlic, onion powder, allspice, and black pepper in a blender and blend on high for 3 minutes, or until smooth. Pour the sauce into a saucepan over medium-high heat and whisk to combine. Bring to a boil, then lower the heat and simmer, uncovered, for 30 minutes, or until the sauce has reduced by about half.

Let the sauce cool to room temperature, then refrigerate for 2 hours before use. The sauce can be stored in an airtight container in the refrigerator for up to 2 weeks.

2½ cups blanched almond flour

1 cup arrowroot powder

¼ cup coconut sugar

2 eggs, chilled

3 tablespoons cold water

½ teaspoon fine sea salt

4 tablespoons palm shortening, chilled

basic pie pastry

To make the pie dough, combine the almond flour, arrowroot, coconut sugar, eggs, water, and salt in a food processor. Process for 10 seconds, or until combined. Add the palm shortening, spacing out where the tablespoons are dropped into the dough. Pulse 4 or 5 times, until pea-size bits of dough form.

Gather the dough into a tight ball and flatten it into a disk. Wrap tightly and freeze for 1 hour.

Transfer the dough to a 9-inch pie plate and press it into the bottom and up the sides of the plate, using the palms of your hands to ensure the crust is even throughout. Press together any breaks in the dough, then crimp or flute the edges with your fingers.

To partially bake the crust, cut a round of parchment paper to fit the bottom of the crust and fill with pie weights or dried beans. Bake at 325°F for 10 minutes, remove the weights and parchment paper, and bake for 5 minutes more, or until the crust is golden. Cool completely on a wire rack.

make it ahead To make the dough up to 2 days in advance, skip the freezer step and refrigerate the disk tightly wrapped. The dough can also be frozen for up to 6 months. Thaw the dough overnight in the refrigerator before using. If the dough cracks or seems dry, wet your hands a bit to press the dough into the pie plate.

tidbits Substitute 3 tablespoons grass-fed unsalted butter or ghee (page 325) for the palm shortening.

Omit the coconut sugar for savory dishes such as the Mummy Dogs (page 214) or to use for a potpie.

blackening seasoning

MAKES ABOUT
7 TABLESPOONS

6 teaspoons sweet paprika

4 teaspoons fine sea salt

2 teaspoons onion powder

2 teaspoons dried oregano

2 teaspoons ground cumin

2 teaspoons chili powder

2 teaspoons freshly ground
black pepper

1 teaspoon dried thyme

1 teaspoon cayenne pepper

Combine the paprika, salt, onion powder, oregano, cumin, chili powder, black pepper, thyme, and cayenne in a small bowl and mix well. Store in an airtight jar in a cool, dry place for up to 6 months.

blender bread

MAKES 1 LOAF

8 eggs

1 cup almond milk (page 320), or store-bought unsweetened almond milk

4 teaspoons apple cider vinegar

3 cups (about 450g) whole raw cashews

2 teaspoons baking soda

1 teaspoon fine sea salt

7 tablespoons coconut flour

Place a heatproof dish filled with 2 inches of water on the bottom rack of the oven and preheat the oven to 325°F. Lightly grease a 10 by 4½-inch loaf pan with ghee (page 325) or coconut oil. Line the bottom and sides of the pan with parchment paper so the ends hang over the sides.

Combine the eggs, almond milk, vinegar, cashews, baking soda, and salt in a high-speed blender and process on low speed for 15 seconds. Scrape down the sides and then process on high for 30 seconds, or until very smooth. Add the coconut flour and blend again for 30 seconds. If the batter is too thick to blend, add up to 2 tablespoons water until it is moving easily through the blender. Transfer the batter to the prepared loaf pan.

Bake for 60 to 70 minutes, until a toothpick inserted into the center of the bread comes out clean.

Allow the bread to cool in the pan for 30 minutes, then gently remove the loaf using the parchment paper overhangs and allow to cool on a wire rack before serving or storing. Store the loaf tightly wrapped in the refrigerator for up to 5 days.

tidbits Be sure to use the suggested pan size for best results.

1¼ cups (about 185g) whole raw cashews

¾ cup water

1½ tablespoons freshly squeezed lemon juice

¾ teaspoon fine sea salt

¾ teaspoon apple cider vinegar

cashew cream

Use this in place of heavy cream in creamy soups or casseroles.

Place the cashews in a bowl and cover them with cold water. Cover the bowl and soak for 4 hours.

Drain and rinse the cashews. Transfer them to a high-speed blender and add the water, lemon juice, salt, and vinegar. Blend on high until the mixture is very smooth. Cover and refrigerate for 2 hours before using, or for up to 3 days.

MAKES 5 CUPS

1 cup (about 150g) whole raw cashews

3 cups water

2 teaspoons light-colored raw honey (optional)

¼ teaspoon fine sea salt

cashew milk

Put the cashews in a bowl and cover them with cold water. Cover the bowl and soak for 4 hours.

Drain and rinse the cashews. Transfer them to a blender and add the water, honey, and salt. Blend on low speed for 30 seconds, then on high speed for 1 to 2 minutes, until creamy. Pour the liquid through a fine-mesh sieve to remove any large fragments. Use immediately, or store in an airtight container in the refrigerator for up to 5 days.

MAKES ABOUT 1 CUP

1½ cups packed fresh flat-leaf parsley leaves

½ cup packed fresh cilantro leaves

2 tablespoons fresh oregano leaves

4 cloves garlic

¾ cup extra-virgin olive oil

¼ cup red wine vinegar

¾ teaspoon dried red pepper flakes

½ teaspoon fine sea salt

¼ teaspoon freshly ground black pepper

chimichurri sauce

Combine the parsley, cilantro, oregano, and garlic in a food processor. Pulse 3 or 4 times, until everything is chopped. Pour in the olive oil and vinegar and pulse twice to incorporate. Season with the red pepper flakes, salt, and pepper. Although the sauce is best served fresh, it will keep in an airtight container in the refrigerator for up to 2 days.

1 pound grass-fed unsalted
butter

ghee

Cut each of the sticks of butter into quarters and place them in a large
saucepan. Melt the butter over medium-high heat, stirring occasionally
to speed the process. It should take about 4 minutes to melt completely.

Bring the melted butter to a boil, then reduce the heat to medium-low to
keep it at a low simmer. White foam will appear on the top of the liquid
but will dissipate. Continue simmering for 10 to 12 minutes, until the
creamy white milk fat rises to the top. Carefully skim the white layer
off the top and discard; you should be left with an opaque golden liquid
below and some solid bits at the bottom of the pan.

Raise the heat back up to medium and simmer again for 3 to 5 minutes,
until any remaining milk solids have fallen to the bottom of the pan and
browned slightly. Be careful not to let them burn or your ghee will have
a burned taste.

Set aside to cool to room temperature, then pour the ghee through a fine-
mesh sieve into a clean airtight jar. Ghee can be used immediately in its
melted state, stored in the refrigerator to become solid, or stored at room
temperature for up to 1 month.

MAKES ABOUT ¾ CUP

½ cup cream of tartar

¼ cup baking soda

2 tablespoons arrowroot
powder

grain-free baking powder

Most commercial baking powders contain aluminum and cornstarch.
This homemade version allows you to control the ingredients and is
quick to make.

Mix together the cream of tartar, baking soda, and arrowroot powder.
Store in an airtight container at room temperature for up to 6 months.

6 eggs, beaten

1 cup almond milk
(page 320) or store-bought
unsweetened almond milk

6 tablespoons coconut flour

½ cup arrowroot powder

2 tablespoons melted ghee
(page 325), plus more for
cooking

½ teaspoon fine sea salt

grain-free wraps

Combine the eggs, almond milk, coconut flour, arrowroot powder, ghee, and salt in a blender. Blend on low for 15 seconds, then let the batter sit for 5 minutes. Blend on high for 15 seconds more.

Heat an 8-inch crepe pan or well-seasoned griddle to medium-high heat. Melt a small amount of ghee in the pan and spread it all over. Ladle ¼ cup of the batter onto the hot pan and quickly spread it into a paper-thin 8-inch circle with the back of the ladle or by turning the pan quickly with your wrist. Fill in any holes with a drop of batter. Cook for 45 seconds, until the sides start to lift, then gently flip the wrap. Cook for 30 seconds on the other side. As the wraps are ready, stack them on a plate and repeat the steps until all of the batter is used, greasing the pan between wraps when needed. Let cool before serving.

The wraps will keep in the refrigerator for up to 5 days or in the freezer for up to 6 months. Place a piece of parchment paper between wraps and store in a resealable bag. Thaw in the refrigerator for 2 hours prior to using.

tidbits A shallow, well-seasoned crepe pan works best for this recipe, or use a large flat griddle to make multiple wraps at a time. Make sure to keep them very thin, and do not try to flip them until the sides start to lift.

MAKES 2 CUPS

1 cup mayonnaise
(page 328)

½ cup full-fat coconut milk

¼ cup fresh flat-leaf parsley,
chopped

2 cloves garlic, crushed

2 tablespoons chopped
fresh chives

2 tablespoons chopped
fresh dill

4 teaspoons freshly
squeezed lemon juice

½ teaspoon onion powder

½ teaspoon fine sea salt

herb ranch dressing

Combine the mayonnaise, coconut milk, parsley, garlic, chives, dill, lemon juice, onion powder, and salt in a bowl. Whisk together until well combined. Serve immediately or store in an airtight container in the refrigerator for up to 5 days.

4 pounds mixed bones
(see Tidbits)

2 tablespoons extra-virgin
olive oil (optional)

Fine sea salt and freshly
ground black pepper
(optional)

4 carrots, cleaned and
halved

2 ribs celery (with leaves),
halved

1 large yellow onion,
quartered

1 bunch flat-leaf parsley

4 cloves garlic, crushed

1 tablespoon apple cider
vinegar

homemade stock

Homemade bone broth, or stock, not only makes the most delicious soups, it is also wonderful for sipping on daily. It is easily digestible, helps heal the lining of your gut, and contains valuable nutrients. The key to getting a good gel to your broth is not filling the pot with too much water; add just enough to cover the bones. This recipe can be used with whatever type of bones you'd like: beef, chicken, or turkey.

If the bones are raw, drizzle them with the olive oil and toss with a generous pinch of salt and pepper. Roast in an oven set to 400°F for 20 minutes. Transfer the bones and any juices from the pan to a stockpot or slow cooker insert. Add the carrots, celery, onion, parsley, garlic, and vinegar.

Fill the stockpot or slow cooker with water until it just covers the bones. Set the pot or the slow cooker to high heat and bring to a boil.

Once the liquid is simmering, skim off any foam at the top. Simmer for 24 to 48 hours. Strain out the solids and skim any fat from the top. Allow to cool to room temperature before storing. Store in jars in the refrigerator for use within 1 week or freeze for up to 6 months.

tidbits I freeze stock in silicone muffin molds, which makes it easy to pop out just what I need. They defrost more quickly, too.

For beef stock, use a mix of marrowbones and bones with a little meat on them, such as oxtail, short ribs, or knuckle bones.

For poultry, use a mix of backs, legs, and feet.

To substitute store-bought broth, use a low-sodium variety.

ketchup

MAKES 2 CUPS

1 tablespoon coconut oil

½ yellow onion, halved

1 clove garlic, crushed into a paste

3¼ cups tomato puree

½ cup light-colored raw honey

⅓ cup white vinegar

1 tablespoon tomato paste

½ teaspoon fine sea salt

8 whole cloves

10 whole allspice berries

Heat the coconut oil in a deep skillet or saucepan over medium heat. Add the onion and garlic and sauté for 5 minutes, or until fragrant. Add the tomato puree, honey, vinegar, tomato paste, salt, cloves, and allspice berries and bring to a boil. Reduce the heat to medium-low and simmer, uncovered, for 40 minutes, or until the sauce has thickened and reduced by half. Remove the onion, cloves, and allspice berries.

Let the ketchup cool to room temperature, then refrigerate for 2 hours before use. The ketchup can be stored in an airtight container in the refrigerator for up to 2 weeks.

mayonnaise

MAKES ¾ CUP

1 egg yolk

1 teaspoon freshly squeezed lemon juice

1 teaspoon white vinegar

½ teaspoon fine sea salt

¼ teaspoon Dijon mustard

¾ cup macadamia nut oil

Combine the egg yolk, lemon juice, vinegar, salt, and mustard in a small blender or mini food processor and blend on low until combined. With the blender on low, begin adding the oil 1 drop at a time. When the mixture begins to thicken, add the remaining oil in a slow, steady stream with the blender still running, until all of the oil has been incorporated. Refrigerate for 2 hours before use, or store in the refrigerator, tightly covered, for up to 3 days.

tidbits Macadamia nut oil is used for its slightly sweet and mild flavor, but other oils, such as olive, avocado, or almond, can be substituted.

A small blender or mini food processor is essential for this method. But mayonnaise can also be made by hand. Combine the egg yolk, lemon juice, vinegar, salt, and mustard in a bowl and whisk to combine. Add ¼ cup of the oil, ½ teaspoon at a time, whisking vigorously. Gradually add the remaining ½ cup oil in a slow, steady stream, whisking constantly, for 5 to 7 minutes until thick. Alternatively, many find that using an immersion blender in a tall, slender container works well.

moroccan spiced jam

MAKES ¾ CUP

2 tablespoons extra-virgin olive oil

1 shallot, peeled and thinly sliced

2 ounces pitted dates, chopped

¾ cup chicken stock (page 327)

1 teaspoon apple cider vinegar

1 teaspoon freshly squeezed lemon juice

½ teaspoon ground coriander

½ teaspoon ground cinnamon

¼ teaspoon ground cumin

¼ teaspoon ground ginger

Heat the olive oil in a saucepan over medium-high heat. Add the shallot and dates and sauté for 2 to 3 minutes, until the shallots are translucent and the dates are softened. Pour in the chicken stock and stir continuously to deglaze the pan. Add the vinegar, lemon juice, coriander, cinnamon, cumin, and ginger and simmer for 15 minutes, or until thickened. Keep warm until ready to serve. Store in an airtight container in the refrigerator for up to 5 days.

pickled onions

MAKES ½ CUP

1 cup water

1 cup apple cider vinegar

2 teaspoons coconut sugar

1 teaspoon fine sea salt

1 teaspoon black peppercorns

1 large red onion, halved and thinly sliced

Combine the water, vinegar, coconut sugar, salt, and peppercorns in a large saucepan and bring to a boil. Put the onion into a large jar and pour in the hot liquid. Allow the onion to cool to room temperature before closing tightly and cooling completely in the refrigerator before using. Store in the fridge for up to 2 weeks.

8 eggs

½ cup almond milk
(page 320) or cashew milk
(page 324)

1 tablespoon apple cider
vinegar

3 cups (about 450g) whole
raw cashews

½ cup arrowroot powder

¼ cup coconut flour

2 teaspoons baking soda

1 teaspoon fine sea salt

1 egg yolk

1 tablespoon water

2 tablespoons poppy seeds

poppy seed hamburger buns

Place a heatproof dish filled with 2 inches of water on the bottom rack of the oven. Preheat the oven to 325°F. Lightly grease the inside of ten 3-inch English muffin rings with ghee (page 325) or coconut oil and place them on a baking sheet lined with parchment paper.

Place the eggs, almond milk, vinegar, cashews, arrowroot, coconut flour, baking soda, salt, egg yolk, and water in a high-speed blender and process on low for 15 seconds. Scrape down the sides and process on high for 15 to 30 seconds, until very smooth.

Fill each ring one-half full with batter and sprinkle the tops with poppy seeds. Bake for 20 to 25 minutes, until a toothpick inserted into the center of the buns comes out clean. Allow the buns to cool on the baking sheet for 15 minutes, then gently press them out of the rings from the bottom. Allow to cool on a wire rack before serving, or store in an airtight container in the freezer for up to 6 months. Defrost in the refrigerator overnight before using.

2 (13.5-ounce) cans full-fat coconut milk

2 teaspoons light-colored raw honey

whipped coconut cream

Be sure to place the cans of coconut milk in the refrigerator 2 days before you want to make this. I suggest chilling more than one can in case there isn't enough cream on top, which can often happen.

Chill a glass or metal bowl in the freezer along with the beaters or whisk attachment for at least 30 minutes.

Carefully remove the coconut milk from the fridge. Scoop off the cream that has risen to the top and place in the chilled bowl. Save the thinner, opaque coconut milk for shakes or other uses. Beat the cream on high speed until peaks form, about 5 minutes. Drizzle the honey in and beat until incorporated. Place the bowl of whipped cream in the fridge for 20 minutes, then beat it again right before serving.

Store in an airtight container in the refrigerator for up to 3 days. Beat on high speed prior to serving.

tidbit Some brands have less cream than others. Be sure to buy full-fat coconut milk, and I suggest Native Forest, Organic Thai Kitchen, or Whole Foods 365 Organic brands for the best cream content.

1 cup (about 150g) whole raw cashews

1½ cups full-fat coconut milk

⅓ cup melted expeller-pressed coconut oil

¼ cup pure maple syrup

1 ounce raw cacao butter, melted (about 3 tablespoons)

½ teaspoon pure vanilla extract

Pinch of fine sea salt

whipped cream

Raw cacao butter gives this structure and causes it to melt in your mouth. Using expeller-pressed coconut oil here is important so the coconut flavor doesn't overwhelm the taste. Mix in 1 cup gently mashed raspberries or strawberries to make a fruity cream filling, or blend in 2 tablespoons natural cocoa powder before chilling.

Put the cashews in a bowl and cover them with water. Cover the bowl and soak for 4 hours.

Drain the cashews and transfer them to a blender. Add the coconut milk, coconut oil, maple syrup, cacao butter, vanilla extract, and salt. Blend on high for 60 seconds, or until very smooth. Transfer the mixture to the bowl of a stand mixer or a large glass bowl. Cover and refrigerate for at least 6 hours or up to 3 days.

In a stand mixer fitted with the whisk attachment, or using an electric handheld mixer, beat the cream until it holds soft peaks when the beaters are lifted out. Serve immediately.

The whipped cream can be stored in the refrigerator for up to 5 days; just rewhip before serving. It can be stored in the freezer, tightly sealed, for up to 3 months. Defrost in the refrigerator overnight, then rewhip before serving. Leftover whipped cream can be used in coffee, to frost a cake, on top of pancakes or waffles, or spread on top of scones. I also love to dip fresh fruit in it.

conversion charts

NUT FLOURS

1 tablespoon = 5g

¼ cup = 25g

⅓ cup = 30g

½ cup = 50g

1 cup = 100g

COCONUT FLOUR AND ARROWROOT POWDER

1 tablespoon = 7g

¼ cup = 30g

⅓ cup = 40g

½ cup = 60g

1 cup = 130g

PALM SHORTENING

1 tablespoon = 12g

¼ cup = 45g

⅓ cup = 65g

½ cup = 90g

1 cup = 180g

WHOLE RAW CASHEWS

¼ cup = 35g

⅓ cup = 49g

½ cup = 70g

¾ cup = 105g

1 cup = 150g

DRY WEIGHT MEASUREMENTS

1 oz = 28g

2 oz = 57g

3 oz = 85g

4 oz = 113g

8 oz = 227g

12 oz = 340g

16 oz = 454g

2.2 lb = 1kg

LIQUID OR VOLUME MEASUREMENTS

1 teaspoon = 5ml

1 tablespoon = 15ml

¼ cup = 59ml

⅓ cup = 79ml

½ cup = 118ml

⅔ cup = 158ml

¾ cup = 178ml

1 cup = 237ml

1 pint (2 cups) = 473ml

2 pints (4 cups) = 946ml

MEASURING EQUIVALENTS

1 tablespoons = 3 teaspoons

⅛ cup = 2 tablespoons

¼ cup = 4 tablespoons

⅓ cup = 5 tablespoons plus 1 teaspoon

½ cup = 8 tablespoons

¾ cup = 12 tablespoons

1 cup = 48 teaspoons

1 cup = 16 tablespoons

8 fluid ounces = 1 cup

1 pint = 2 cups

1 quart = 2 pints

4 cups = 1 quart

1 gallon = 4 quarts

16 ounces = 1 pound

gratitude

My readers: As always, my first and deepest gratitude goes to my readers and the healthy-eating community. I hear your recipe requests, strive to improve on your critiques, and am overjoyed by your affirmations. I would not be creating these cookbooks if it weren't for you, so thank you for your continued support and enthusiasm for my work.

My family: I am so fortunate to have a family that has supported my endeavors since day one and always pushes me to strive for greatness. Thank you to my husband, Ryan, and to my boys, Asher and Easton, for inspiring me to re-create these memories for us to share together for years to come, and to my mom and my grandmother, for sharing stories and memories of their own childhood traditions.

Sydney: I feel so lucky that I get to wake up in the morning and head into the kitchen to test recipes. I know not everyone shares that passion, but my culinary assistant and right-hand gal, Sydney Steele, is every bit as enthusiastic about it as I am. She understands the thrill of nailing a recipe on the first try and puts up with me asking her to retest something dozens of times with only minor changes to perfect it (ahem, the buttercream frosting and red velvet cake). Plus, she brings so much joy into the kitchen. I am so grateful for her assistance on this book; it would be impossible for these recipes to be as bulletproof as they are without Sydney's help.

Kari: Thank you to my wonderful agent, Kari Stuart, for believing in me and in this book, and for helping me find the perfect publisher for my work. I know I can trust that she is looking out for me and handling the rest of the details, which lets me focus more fully on writing and creating.

The Ten Speed team: I could not have put this book together without my amazing publisher, Ten Speed Press, and my lovely editor, Julie Bennett. This was my first time working with them and the process has been a dream. Thank you to Emma Campion, Ashley Lima, Kaitlin Ketchum, and the rest of the creative team for dreaming up each celebration with me and helping me execute the many moving pieces to make it happen. I happily relinquished much of the control I was used to having into their very capable and talented hands. Thank you to David Hawk and Michele Crim and the entire Penguin Random House marketing and publicity team for working so hard to make this book known and get it out to the public.

The Brooks Group Public Relations: I'm honored to be part of your roster and have so enjoyed working with your team over the past couple of years. Thank you for working with the Ten Speed team and handling the promotion of this book so exceptionally well.

The creative team: The concept of this book would not be what it is without the brilliant work of the photography team. I had so much fun with them on our weeks of photo shoots and was sad to see it end. Thank you to the extraordinary Erin Kunkel, for bringing my food and vision to life on the page and capturing such beautiful images of my family and friends, even while risking your life on the rascal to get the perfect shot! Thank you to my talented food stylists, Lillian Kang and Valerie Aikman-Smith, for venturing into the unfamiliar world of grain-free cooking and baking and making the food look more beautiful than I could have imagined. And thanks to my prop stylist, Glen Jenkins, for finding such unique tableware and decor to make each party feel special. I have a hard time trimming down my recipe lists when I'm trying to equip my readers with everything they need, and these wonderful stylists gracefully took on the ambitious shot list.

My recipe testers: There is a big group to whom I am forever grateful for testing each and every recipe in this book on their own time and dime. I am adamant about having my recipes tested in the home kitchens of readers prior to publishing them to ensure everything can be re-created successfully by novice cooks as well as seasoned chefs. The testers' valuable feedback, critiques, and praise helped make these recipes perfect. And special thanks to Rob and his family of eager eaters, who have been my rock-star testers since the first book.

recipe index

special diets index

	EGG-FREE	NUT-FREE	NIGHTSHADE-FREE	SCD/GAPS*
Apple Parsnip Soup Shooters	◆	◆	◆	
Oysters with Champagne-Pomegranate Mignonette	◆	◆	◆	◆
Prosciutto-Wrapped Glazed Shrimp	◆	◆		
Spinach Artichoke Dip with Crudités				◆
Thai Chicken Meatballs with Tamarind Chili Sauce	◆	◆		
Crab-Stuffed Mushrooms			◆	◆
Champagne Chocolate Strawberries	◆	◆	◆	
Holiday Gimlet	◆	◆	◆	◆
NYE 75	◆	◆	◆	◆
Sweet-and-Sour-Meatballs				◆
Buffalo Wings with Herb Ranch Dressing	◆	◆		◆
Cauliflower Buffalo Bites	◆	◆		
Carnitas on Tostones	◆	◆		
Green Chile Chicken Soup	◆	◆		
Whoopie Pies		◆	◆	
My Heart Beets For You Smoothie	◆		◆	◆
Cupid's Arrow Pancakes			◆	
Be Mine Pizza	◆	◆		
Wedge Salad with Herb Ranch Dressing		◆		◆
Cabernet-Braised Short Ribs with Parsnip-Turnip Puree	◆	◆		
Chile Garlic Rapini	◆	◆		◆
Salted Caramel-Chocolate Panna Cotta	◆			
Caramel Pecan Sticky Buns			◆	
Asparagus Prosciutto Tart			◆	
Butter Lettuce, Citrus, and Haricots Verts Salad	◆	◆	◆	◆
Lavender Rosemary Leg of Lamb	◆	◆	◆	
Blood Orange Honey Glazed Ham	◆	◆	◆	◆
Sweet Potato Orange Cups	◆		◆	
Carrot Cake	◆	◆	◆	
Lavender Lemonade	◆	◆	◆	◆
Asparagus and Leek Soup with a Poached Egg		◆	◆	
Eggs Benedict Strata				◆
Strawberry Salmon Salad with Poppy Seed Dressing	◆		◆	◆
Lemon Bars		◆	◆	
Ginger Peach Sangria	◆	◆	◆	◆
Knife-and-Fork Pork Ribs	◆	◆		
Tri-Tip with Grilled Vegetables and Chimichurri Sauce	◆	◆		
Baked "Beans"	◆			
Skillet "Corn" Bread			◆	
Peach Cobbler	◆		◆	
Margarita	◆	◆	◆	
Burger Bites	◆	◆		◆
Mini "Corn" Dog Muffins			◆	
AB&J Hand Sandwiches			◆	◆

*SCD (Specific Carbohydrate Diet) and GAPS (Gut and Psychology Syndrome Diet)

	EGG-FREE	NUT-FREE	NIGHTSHADE-FREE	SCD/GAPS*
Fruit Kabobs	◆		◆	◆
Veggie Cups		◆		◆
Chocolate Cake		◆	◆	
Red Velvet Cake		◆	◆	
Nut-Free Yellow Cake		◆	◆	
Yellow Cake			◆	
Strawberry Cake			◆	◆
Vanilla Cake			◆	
Vanilla Buttercream	◆	◆	◆	
Cream Cheese Frosting	◆	◆	◆	
Quick Chocolate Icing	◆	◆	◆	
Heirloom Tomato, Watermelon, and Basil Salad	◆	◆		◆
Grandma's Potato Salad		◆		
BLTA Burger with Special Sauce[+]		◆		◆
Blackened Salmon with Stone-Fruit Salsa	◆	◆		◆
Berry Tart with Vanilla Bean Custard		◆	◆	
Ginger Ale	◆	◆	◆	◆
Smoked Salmon Deviled Eggs		◆	◆	◆
Pesto Deviled Eggs				◆
Avocado Tarragon Deviled Eggs		◆	◆	◆
Truffled Bacon Deviled Eggs		◆		◆
Ahi Tartare on Taro Chips	◆	◆		
Chicken Salad Biscuits			◆	◆
Lemon Lavender Bundt Cakes			◆	
Zabaglione with Berries		◆	◆	◆
Mimosa Bar	◆	◆	◆	◆
Spider Cookies	◆	◆	◆	
Dirt Cups[^]	◆	◆	◆	
Sunbutter Chocolate Cups	◆	◆	◆	
Caramel Apples	◆	◆	◆	
Mummy Dogs			◆	
Witches' Fingers			◆	◆
Curry Pumpkin Soup	◆		◆	
Roasted Autumn Harvest Salad	◆		◆	◆
Butternut Sage Carbonara			◆	◆
Chai-Poached Pears	◆		◆	
Spiced Apple Hot Toddy	◆	◆	◆	◆
Herbed Drop Biscuits			◆	◆
Roasted Garlic Mashed Cauliflower	◆	◆	◆	◆
Cranberry Sauce	◆	◆	◆	◆
Green Bean Casserole with Crispy Shallots	◆		◆	◆
Smoky Candied Bacon Sweet Potatoes	◆			
Roasted Brussels Sprouts with Bacon Jam	◆	◆		
Apple Sausage Stuffing			◆	◆
Roasted Brined Turkey	◆	◆	◆	◆

*SCD (Specific Carbohydrate Diet) and GAPS (Gut and Psychology Syndrome Diet)
[+]Grain-free rolls not accounted for
[^]Omit cookie crumble for egg-free

	EGG-FREE	NUT-FREE	NIGHTSHADE-FREE	SCD/GAPS*
Maple Pumpkin Pie			◆	◆
Apple Pie			◆	
Chocolate Pecan Tart			◆	
Pumpkin Spice Latte	◆		◆	
Cinnamon Rolls	◆		◆	
Sausage Breakfast Casserole		◆		
Gingerbread Latte	◆		◆	
Persimmon Prosciutto Salad	◆	◆	◆	◆
Creamed Spinach	◆		◆	◆
Vegetable Bacon Parcels	◆	◆	◆	
Stuffing-Filled Turkey Breast			◆	◆
Whole Roasted Branzino with Fennel and Tomatoes	◆	◆		◆
Rosemary Garlic Rib Roast	◆	◆	◆	
Cranberry Gingerbread Cake			◆	
Mulled Wine	◆	◆	◆	
Granny Sarella's Panettone			◆	
Gingerbread House			◆	
Thumbprint Cookies	◆		◆	◆
Sunbutter Buckeyes	◆	◆	◆	
Gingersnap Cookies	◆		◆	
Granny Sarella's Biscotti			◆	
Cutout Cookies			◆	
Christmas Fudge	◆		◆	
Peppermint Hot Cocoa	◆		◆	
Marshmallows	◆	◆	◆	
Eggnog			◆	◆
Almond Milk	◆		◆	◆
Barbecue Sauce	◆	◆		◆
Basic Pie Pastry			◆	
Blackening Seasoning	◆	◆		◆
Blender Bread			◆	◆
Cashew Cream	◆		◆	◆
Cashew Milk	◆		◆	◆
Chimichurri Sauce	◆	◆		◆
Ghee	◆	◆	◆	◆
Grain-Free Baking Powder	◆	◆	◆	
Grain-Free Wraps			◆	
Herb Ranch Dressing		◆	◆	◆
Homemade Stock	◆	◆	◆	◆
Ketchup	◆	◆		◆
Mayonnaise		◆	◆	◆
Moroccan Spiced Jam	◆	◆	◆	◆
Pickled Onions	◆	◆	◆	
Poppy Seed Hamburger Buns			◆	
Whipped Coconut Cream	◆	◆	◆	◆
Whipped Cream	◆		◆	

*SCD (Specific Carbohydrate Diet) and GAPS (Gut and Psychology Syndrome Diet)

index

Copyright © 2016 by Simple Writing Holdings, LLC
Photographs copyright © 2016 by Erin Kunkel

All rights reserved.
Published in the United States by Ten Speed Press, an imprint of the
Crown Publishing Group, a division of Penguin Random House LLC, New York.
www.crownpublishing.com
www.tenspeed.com

Ten Speed Press and the Ten Speed Press colophon are registered trademarks of
Penguin Random House LLC.

Library of Congress Cataloging-in-Publication Data is on file with the publisher.

Hardcover ISBN: 978-1-60774-942-4
eBook ISBN: 978-1-60774-943-1

Printed in China

Design by Ashley Lima
Food styling by Lillian Kang and Valerie Aikman-Smith
Food styling assistance by Amanda Anselmino, Abby Stolfo, and Nicole Twohy
Prop styling by Glenn Jenkins
Prop styling assistance by Jordin Riley and Bill Samios
Photography assistance by David Bornfriend and François Lebeau
Hair and makeup by Lindsay Skog

10 9 8 7 6 5 4 3 2 1

First Edition